ORIENTATION TO
COLLEGE LEARNING
—A REAPPRAISAL

ORIENTATION TO COLLEGE LEARNING —A REAPPRAISAL

Report of a Conference on
Introduction of Entering Students
to the Intellectual Life of the College,

Edited by Nicholas C. Brown

AMERICAN COUNCIL ON EDUCATION • *Washington, D.C.*

87620

PRINTED IN THE UNITED STATES OF AMERICA

FOREWORD

IN RECENT years, the Council's Commission on the College Student has tried to bring into focus the concern of many institutions with the initiation of students to college life. What impressions does the entering student receive in the first week, the first semester, and the first year of college? Do these impressions fulfill his legitimate expectations? Do they confirm his finest hopes and elicit his best efforts? Or do they sometimes blunt his keenest interests and, in fact, seem to run counter to the aims of the college itself?

This is a report of a conference, held at Princeton University, October 31–November 2, 1960, addressed to these general questions. The Council hopes that this publication will stimulate many institutions to give serious consideration to ways in which they can more effectively introduce entering students to the intellectual life on their campuses. The Princeton conference on this topic was the second of two regional conferences sponsored by the commission. It was held because of the interest generated by the first conference at the University of Notre Dame in February 1959, of which no report was published.

The Council gratefully acknowledges its indebtedness to the conference participants, who gave their thoughtful attention to this problem and who, in so doing, provided the basis for this report. The Council also expresses its gratitude to the Ford Foundation for the funds that made both the conference and the report possible.

ARTHUR S. ADAMS, *President*
American Council on Education

June 30, 1961

PREFACE

THE PURPOSE of this conference was to explore more effective ways of introducing students to the intellectual aims and values of the college. There are as many freshman orientation programs as there are colleges. Not all of these programs, of course, are formally planned. Of those which are, many are confined to the two- to six-day variety of Orientation Week, which often serves more as an administrative convenience than as an introduction to an academic experience.

A basic task of the college is to encourage the student increasingly to accept responsibility for his own learning. Few colleges, however, have devoted attention to the fact that most entering freshmen have crossed the threshold of a new world, that they expect college to be different from high school, and that they are receptive to meaningful indications that it *is* different.

Discussions in the Commission on the College Student have suggested that the colleges tend to ignore the development of attitudes of beginning students toward the institution's intellectual values. The commission believes that this may be a reflection of a gap in the understanding by some faculty members of student backgrounds, objectives, and expectations, and by some students of what the faculty members hope will take place. The commission believes that clearer understanding between faculty members and students of their common goals is essential.

As an exploratory step toward the solution of some of these problems, the commission invited the guests of this conference to join with its members in considering some of the practical means of introducing entering students to the intellectual life of the college.

WILSON H. ELKINS, *Chairman*
Commission on the College Student

CONTENTS

LIST OF TABLES

LIST OF FIGURES

THE CLIMATE OF LEARNING

MASON W. GROSS
President,
Rutgers—The State University

E VERY SPRING I have the pleasure of meeting some of the new
and brighter students who have indicated their intention of
entering Rutgers in the fall, and I have always wished that I had
some kind of magical gift that would enable me to say just the
right thing to these new students so that, through the summer,
their sense of excitement about entering college would intensify
steadily and by September they would be "r'aring to go." My
greatest worry today about the entering freshman is that he may be
inclined to take the whole notion of going to college as something
routine and ordinary because there are so many of him, and that
the special significance of this step may be lost. Therefore any
contribution that I can make toward keeping the excitement of
this event alive is something very dear to my heart.

The purpose of this conference is to consider orientation programs and the like. Before we can decide, however, what would
constitute a good orientation program, we must, I assume, tackle
the vastly more difficult problem of determining the objectives
toward which the students are to be oriented. I take it, therefore,
that my role tonight is to suggest to you certain attitudes, habits,
or values which we would like to see our future students acquire
as they enter college and gradually get used to its ways. Let me
say initially that there are plenty of answers to this problem. Every
year I give a certain number of high school commencement talks,
and every year I greet the entire incoming freshman class, and I
always speak on the importance of the step that is now being
taken. I talk about the college student's duty to assume the initiative now in his education because the only educated man is the

1

self-educated man, about the difference between training and education, about the pursuit of truth and the necessity for self-criticism, and so on, *ad nauseam*. Fortunately, on neither occasion is there anybody listening. Thanks to the American custom of having the high school commencement speaker placed with his back to the graduating class, the students are able to sit out the address, waving to their friends and relatives in the audience. And by the time I get to the incoming freshman, he has had so much advice that he can't take on any more.

But there is a further difficulty in trying to get any point across to an audience of this sort. At most high school commencements the speaker is aware that a large portion of his audience is not going on to college and therefore has no interest at all in what he is trying to say. Unfortunately, this is almost equally true if one talks to an entire freshman class. If one were really to try to fascinate them by a discourse on "The Climate of Learning," he would quickly find that the reasons that have prompted them to go to college have little or nothing to do with any concept of learning as such. This is not the time for me to try to analyze why the various elements in an American student body today find themselves as college students, but I assume you will agree that the answer would be extremely complicated. Some small and highly selective colleges may be able to achieve a degree of uniformity of motivation, but I suspect that any admissions list will include some students who are there for purely social reasons; some, for purely economic reasons; some, for family reasons; and some, for no reason at all. Because of the role which American colleges are called upon to play in our society, our attitude to all such groups is hospitable and hopeful; we shall make converts from each group, and others will soon drop out. But if we try to capture the imaginations of all these several groups by a single orientation speech or even program, we are probably attempting the impossible. It takes me a whole year to try to figure out why the students who have enrolled in my philosophy course are in fact there. To extend speculation to an entire freshman class is a forbidding notion.

Let me say quickly, however, that in any freshman class there are also students who are genuinely there in the interest of learning. This is the key group, and our success or failure with them is the truest measure of our success or failure as a college. If this group is large enough and thrives during its college years, it can determine the whole atmosphere of the college. Let us, therefore, turn our attention to the needs and demands of this group.

We must note at once an ambiguity in our terminology. We are using the familiar term "learning" as if it had one clear and distinct meaning. Almost any student, if asked why he is in college, will answer that he is there for the sake of learning. Here, then, we must distinguish between the notion of learning as a means to some further end and learning as practically an end in itself. A student who is busy learning the essentials of physiology may have in view the further end of getting into medical school, with the still further end of practicing medicine. A student who is learning Spanish irregular verbs may be hoping to be a Spanish scholar; or he may envisage a successful business career in South America; or he may simply be seeking to satisfy a foreign language requirement for a bachelor's degree, which in itself is primarily important to him as an admission ticket to a good but as yet unspecified job. Students of these types probably constitute the great bulk of our student body. But while we must agree that these students are learning, and are in college for the sake of learning, their concept of learning is still that it is a means to a further end, whether that end be clearly envisaged or not. The college curriculum is good if it does actually help them get into medical or law school, and the college degree is worth the effort if it does actually help them get what they believe to be a better job.

At the opposite pole are the students and, of course, the faculty, for whom learning is an end in itself. We must not think of this as too highbrow a notion. A certain young lady I know was recently engaged in filling out an application blank for admission to college and ran into trouble over the question, "Why do you want to go to college?" She had the good taste to reject all the obvious answers as being clichés and finally blurted out: "The only reason I want to go to college is that I like what I am doing now, and I can't imagine stopping at this point." I urged her to write that down at once in the appropriate place on the form, because in essence that answer showed that she was enjoying learning for its own sake and saw no point in trying to dream up any other reason. I think she will get by the admissions officer. For her a college is a place where you learn, and learning is a self-justifying process.

We have here also the clue, although I probably should not reveal it, as to why so many able men on college faculties find no problem whatsoever in turning down vastly more lucrative jobs outside the academic world. They are simply the people for whom learning itself is the source of satisfaction, rather than any further ends served by the results of that learning. This devotion to learning is systematically exploited by our society.

Let us agree, then, that a certain percentage of our student body and the great majority of our faculty are motivated by a love of learning in and for itself. The next question is what, if anything, we can mean by the phrase "The Climate of Learning." We must get from "learning" as a participle to "learning" as a noun. Here again we make a distinction, although it is a bit harder to formulate than the earlier one. When we speak of someone as being a "learned" man, we mean something more than the mere fact that he has learned many things even though we may believe that he has learned for the sheer joy of learning. To borrow a phrase out of context from Mr. Whitehead, "Mere scraps of information have nothing to do with it." I had a cousin who must have memorized, out of sheer joy, the timetables of every railroad in the United States and thereby underscored Whitehead's next comment: "The merely well-informed man is the worst bore on God's earth."

I think we can readily agree that the concept of learning must involve essentially the notion of intellectuality and the activity of an analytical and critical mind. The scholar who can give us a new edition of Sophocles is not merely a man who has accumulated more information about the texts of Sophocles than anyone else, but one who can so sift and organize this information that it sheds light on the texts themselves. But here again we have something of a problem. Whenever we set about to give a satisfactory definition of learning and the learned man, we usually try to set it up in such a way as to exclude the mere pedant. I am not sure that we can do this. Perhaps I have a sneaking affection for the pedant. I should confess to you that I am probably the only man who knows for sure which of the two forms of the conjunction, *ut* and *uti*, Vitruvius uses more frequently in the first book of his work on architecture. I am going to keep that information to myself, and if anyone wants to share my knowledge, he can jolly well go and count for himself. And so I will defend the pedants, if only on the ground that too often an insistence on precise and accurate scholarship is dismissed as pedantry by the lazy.

Nevertheless, the concern about pedantry brings up another element in our conception of learning which we must not ignore, and that is the element of value. The learned man not only knows a great deal and has organized and analyzed it with a clear intellectual judgment, he has also evaluated it. You may think that I am now confusing the learned man with the wise man. I will agree that not all wise men are learned, but I doubt whether I would agree that a man can be truly called learned unless he shares with the wise man that ability to discriminate and evaluate what is important and worthwhile.

But this notion of value brings me to what I consider the most significant element in the definition of the learned man: whatever his subject matter may be, he is head over heels in love with it. In other words, we must classify him as Alcibiades insisted we must classify Socrates, as a lover. And he is as romantic a lover as you will ever meet. The poet praises not only his mistress, but the air which kisses her cheek, the flowers which are entwined in her hair, and even the fortunate people on whom her casual glance may rest momentarily. But consider, for example, the man of learning in Greek and Latin literature. He loves not only his texts and the beauty of their language—he loves the medieval manuscripts and the various handwritings in which they have come down to us, the incunabula and the smell of ancient leather, the ancient commentators and editors. Names like Bentley and Porson are music to his soul, yes, and even Wilamowitz-Moellendorff.

And surely what is true of the classical scholar is equally true of the historian of art or music, of literature or philosophy. Romance is the very essence of the historian, but the mathematician is the man who most frequently employs romantic terminology. And is this not equally true of the scientist? From Archimedes to

Roger Bacon to the present, the scientist's devotion to truth has been a romantic notion, and Lucretius is its poet. We may recall Whitehead's suggestion that had Shelley not been a great poet, he might have been a great chemist, a suggestion which has been seriously followed up. The idea of discovery is likewise a romantic idea, whether it be a discovery from a peak in Darien or discovery after patient years of search in a laboratory.

But I am being carried away by my insistence on the romantic element in the notion of learning, and I must bring myself back to our topic. This conference has been called a "Conference on the Introduction of Entering Students to the Intellectual Life of the College." And here I am, talking of love and romance instead of the intellect. My defense must be that I am really talking about the same thing, but in somewhat broader terms. What we all want is to introduce the student to the college in such a way that he profits most by his years there, regardless of any further profit that may accrue after he leaves college. I think it would be a great mistake, and utterly false as far as undergraduate experience is concerned, to try to isolate one aspect of college life and label it as intellectual, with the implied suggestion that herein lies all that is worthwhile. Our entering freshman, if he is lucky, will be beginning the four most exciting years of his life. And here we must follow Plato when he tells us so very rightly of the many ways in which our student will fall in love—in love with certainly one and possibly more than one physical body, in love with political and social ideas, in love with scientific notions and objects, in love with beauty itself as an ecstatic vision and with all its varied manifestations. What a curriculum this is, involving all the many sides of the soul and the body too! And yet, as I say, this is what can be predicted for our young student if he is lucky. And it is to Plato again that I can appeal for authority when I insist that the lure of the intellectual life is a romantic one, a more educated form of love, perhaps, but attracting because of its beauty.

I know that the worst breach of good taste one can make on an occasion like this is to justify what one has said by appealing to one's own experience. However, I do want to insist that I am not making all of this up out of whole cloth. My four years as an undergraduate at Cambridge were a glorious romantic whirl, with everything all mixed up. When my best friend and I, he a mad Irishman and a wild drinker, walked solemnly to Heffer's bookstore to buy, not one, but two copies of Kant's *Critique of Pure Reason;* when a fellow oarsman planned with me an Easter vacation in Rome so that we could read Cicero on the edge of the Palatine and follow his steps in the Forum below us; or when I, waiting in a pub to take my turn at a game of darts, first discovered the wonder of the *Phaedrus,* we may have been discovering the intellectual life, but we were doing it as romantics.

And so I insist that in its very essence the idea of learning is a romantic idea, as romantic as casement windows, ivy, and bell towers. If I surprise you by adding to the list fraternities, it is only to remind you that the first American fraternity was Phi Beta Kappa. The caustic tutor with his pipe and an infinite number of matches, the professor beloved for his absent-mindedness, the bull session ranging without interruption from sport to T. S. Eliot and from sex to Augustine, the green lawns and the carefully tended flower beds—all these and many more are the essential trappings of college life, within which the intellectual life will begin to flourish.

But obviously something is wrong, or, with everything so simple, we should not be meeting in conference on this subject. Obviously too many students are not receiving the curriculum that Diotima prescribed. We are therefore met to find ways and means of hurdling the obstacles that seem to be in the way of America's undergraduates today. Let us see what some of these obstacles are.

The first and most obvious difficulty is that the colleges today have to deal with such an enormous number of students. Because of these numbers we in the colleges have had to erect a huge apparatus of admissions officers, deans, catalogues, registrars, physical examinations, and so on. Let's face it. The modern college dean, unlike the older cathedral deans, is not a romantic figure; in fact, he exists largely to ensure that all romance shall be kept within bounds. I have no recommendation to make here except to point out that the prime requisite of every administrative officer whose duties bring him into contact with an entering freshman should be warmth of personality. But this is not the only difficulty that results from numbers. It is hard to be romantic in a crowd.

Romance stirs within the individual soul, and only the miracle of friendship can bring it out. Numbers by their weight tend to depersonalize and thus make romantic aspirations more difficult to encourage. Privacy is essential, at least some of the time, and privacy is daily growing rarer on the campus.

We must also look at the hordes of students to see who they are. In 1900 only 5 percent of the boys and girls between the ages of eighteen and twenty-two were in college. Today that percentage is creeping up to 40. Nearly 40 percent of the graduates of the high schools in New Jersey go on to college today. When you multiply these percentages by the increasing population, you understand why the colleges are facing such pressures. Now, the increasing percentage is undoubtedly both necessary and good. Our society is becoming so complicated that we must have a much larger percentage of people with advanced education, and it is good to know that so many more of our people are discovering that they have the talents which higher education can, and should, develop. But the very fact that our country needs these trained people has caused us to turn our attention increasingly to the practical side of education and to stress it at almost every step of the way, and this, in turn, puts us in danger of turning our educational programs into mere training schools. Undoubtedly a large percentage of our undergraduates have some form of fairly strong motivation, and undoubtedly most of that motivation is strictly practical. The percentage of those who are in college because they wish to pursue learning for its own sake is almost certainly shrinking, although this is not too easy to determine since most students will feel that they should be able to specify a practical motivation, whether it is the real one or not.

And then, of course, we have the Russian system and the presumed Russian success to keep us with our noses to the grindstone. I must state, to be consistent, that I can't help believing that if the Russians really achieve any major intellectual triumphs it will be less because of the Marxist scheme of ideas and regimentation than because the spirit of Dostoevsky and Tolstoy, of Pushkin and Tschaikowsky still burns in Russian breasts. Meanwhile, however, we are being constantly reminded of the insistently practical character of our operations, and federal grants encourage us to direct our research as well as some of our teaching activities along these purely practical lines. But if the demands of practicality are affecting the attitude of the students as well as our own attitude toward the students, they are also affecting the academic mores of the faculty. When a biologist who has spent his life working on protein metabolism and nutrition suddenly learns that his possible solution of a pressing social problem may save an area from communism, he can hardly be blamed for taking time off to do what he can—in fact, it is almost certainly his duty to do so. But meanwhile he is not on the campus exciting students to emulate him.

There is another factor with which I scarcely dare take up your time since it is now mentioned very often. Alongside the practicality of our contemporary studies and the sense of urgency and even danger with which we have grown so familiar, the normal tendency of society not to like criticism and novelty is being reinforced. The intellectual has never been popular because he tends to give serious consideration to alternatives to current mores, whether these alternatives be social, political, religious, or what have you. But the intellectual life is essentially the discovery, contemplation, and evaluation of alternatives, and conformity to any given pattern is its death warrant. You cannot be cautious and romantic at the same time, for romanticism is an adventure into the mysterious unknown.

To list these threats to the intellectual life on the campus is unfortunately not the same thing as to find a solution to them. We are facing problems that have to be solved, and the colleges have to help with their solution. How to accomplish this and still play the role that is uniquely ours, the role of encouraging the life of the intellect, is our unsolved problem today.

One thing, however, is happening today that may counterbalance some of the other forces. In the past, the creative arts have fought shy of the colleges, which were thought to be places where academicism sought to stifle novelty. Today creative writers, painters, sculptors, architects, and musicians are beginning to find a much more congenial spirit on the campuses. In addition, the colleges are beginning to take much more seriously their obligations to the students in matters concerned with culture, as well as to the communities in which they are located. Since I believe, with Plato, that rhythm and music sink deeply into a man's soul and have a profound effect on him, it may be that our romantic can follow the path of the creative arts to the discovery of the intellectual life.

Furthermore, there seems to be a feeling in the air that we are on the verge of new discoveries so profound in their implications as to alter drastically our basic conception of the world and our place in it as human beings. This will force us again to emphasize the basic sciences and the re-examination of scientific concepts in the most fundamental way. And any challenge on this level must be good.

Whenever we talk of the intellectual life or the romantic spirit, we would, I believe, do well to remember Spinoza's equation of the power of the intellect with human freedom. The motto for the intellectual life must be, in Jesus' words, "Ye shall know the truth, and the truth shall make you free." In the last analysis, and on the most practical of practical grounds, the merely practical objectives of education and of learning must yield precedence to the ultimate objectives of learning for its own sake, of beauty for its own sake, and of freedom for its own sake. Not all of the students on any campus, nor even a large number of them, will ever grasp this truth. But if a faculty of free spirits can continue to inspire even a relatively small nucleus of students with a romantic love of learning for its own sake, then the climate of learning on the campus will be salubrious, and the health of the college will be assured.

DISCUSSION

Presiding: WILSON H. ELKINS, *President, University of Maryland*

JOHN W. GUSTAD *(Dean, College of Liberal Arts, Alfred University)*: Dr. Gross, I gather that you are an admirer of Whitehead, as I am. In the light of what you have said, however, I wish you would comment on his statement, "If an education is not useful, what is it?"

DR. GROSS: Well, useful for what? Useful for one's development as a human being? Useful for society in the fullest sense? Or useful for making a better mousetrap? I don't think he ever meant the latter. You can't turn Whitehead into a man advocating education for the immediate, practical goal. No man was more clear in his opposition to this than Whitehead. The two sentences I quoted came from the opening paragraphs of his book *The Aims of Education,* which goes as follows:

Culture is activity of thought, and receptiveness to beauty and humane feeling. Scraps of information have nothing to do with it. A merely well-informed man is the most useless bore on God's earth. What we should aim at producing is men who possess both culture and expert knowledge in some special direction. Their expert knowledge will give them the ground to start from, and their culture will lead them as deep as philosophy and as high as art.

THOMAS MORRISSEY *(President, Student Government Association, University of Maryland):* Sir, with the increase in enrollments, isn't it going to be necessary for the student to assume a greater responsibility for his own education? The college professor is being asked to teach larger and larger classes, and he is simply not able, in most instances, to prod and challenge each student personally. Under these circumstances, doesn't the student himself, if he is at all intellectually motivated, have to accept more initiative than he has in the past?

At our university, we are growing by leaps and bounds; consequently, we have a great number of large classes. It is difficult, if not impossible, for every professor to help each student individually. He has to teach to the mass. However, some of us find it possible, and worthwhile, to meet with a professor occasionally in the evening for an informal discussion. In general, won't students have to seek out the professor or other interested students and visit the library, the laboratory, and the like on their own more and more as enrollments rise?

DR. GROSS: Good students have always taken the initiative in pursuing their education; however, if students were entirely self-propelled, we wouldn't need colleges and faculties. The problem is not merely one of class size.

My own institution has had to resort to large introductory classes. Every college and university with increasing enrollments already has or soon will have some very large classes. But large classes do not always produce the poor results that some faculty members are afraid of and almost expect. On the contrary, sometimes they produce the opposite results. We have discovered that among our best scholars we have some wonderful hams, persons who can stand up before four or five hundred students and really excite them. This is wonderful. It is the kind of excitement that can be engendered in a group of five hundred but not in a group of forty. The large class provides a different kind of atmosphere and requires a different kind of performance. The right kind of teacher can stimulate a large class in a way that it could not otherwise be stimulated at all.

Furthermore, if we save faculty time and money by having large introductory classes for freshmen and sophomores, we should be able to provide small seminars for juniors and seniors when they become engrossed in their fields of concentration and need personal contact and direct inspiration.

Informal contacts between students and faculty members outside class are good; however, as campuses grow and people are scattered several miles apart, such contacts become more difficult to arrange. But almost every faculty member is flattered to be invited to a fraternity house or elsewhere for an evening bull session. There he can roam across any subject area he likes. He is glad not to have any responsibilities, and he has a good time.

There is no doubt that increasing enrollments will force students to assume more responsibility for their own education. The only question is, how shall we motivate them to accept it? How shall we fire them? There are two ways. The first is to hit them on the head with the practical considerations of getting a degree in, let's say, engineering or law and of getting a job. The other is to lure them, not with the reward for grades and credits, but with the romantic excitement of learning itself. A student who has gotten excited by the movement of the Bulgar tribes in Bulgaria in the ninth century finds it a fascinating thing to study in itself. He does not ask that it be useful. The extent to which students do extra reading on their own is a good indication of the worth of the faculty.

WILLIAM GRAHAM COLE (*President, Lake Forest College*): The

thing that troubles me at this point, Dr. Gross, is the lack of attention most of us give to the peer culture, which I think is the most important factor in the climate of learning. So far as our able students are concerned, we don't have much to worry about; these students are self-starters and get along all right. But the predominant mood on most campuses that I know reflects the mood of society as a whole. It is essentially anti-intellectual, essentially bread-and-butter oriented.

Many students who might otherwise be moved to join the group of excited romantics that you are talking about are afraid to exhibit their enthusiasm because of the opinion of their peers. The acceptance and approval of their peers is far more important to them than the acceptance and approval of their mentors. Although this deterrent to learning exists on almost all campuses, we don't do much about it. The faculty bewails and bemoans it, but the faculty hasn't really found an effective way to combat it. No one seems to have discovered the key that unlocks the average student's desire to learn something for its own sake.

This is a condition that deserves very serious attention, particularly as student enrollments become larger and larger. I am not as optimistic as you are that we are going to win out. Unless we do something about the peer culture, I think we shall lose.

DR. GROSS: I think much of what you say is true; however, I think we decry our times a little bit more than we should. We do have terrific pressures toward practicality that are responsible, in large part, for the increased numbers on our campuses. When we look back at the "better" days and bemoan our present situation, we must remember that the small fringe of self-starters once constituted practically the entire student body. We still have the self-starters, and we ought to organize them rather than leave them alone. Perhaps we could thereby strengthen their influence.

I am encouraged, for example, by the increasing activity in art and music at Rutgers. We have developed a choir in which about 275 students will participate this year. This choir has been singing major works with the Philadelphia and two or three other orchestras and has become quite an attraction on the campus. The students fill the gymnasium 3,500 strong to hear it. The members enjoy prestige among their peers, but that is not why they sing. They sing because they like to sing. This is a wonderful thing; it keeps the romantic spirit alive. Building up the prestige of activities like this gradually affects the whole climate of the campus. I agree with you that this is what needs to be done. We must affect and infect the whole campus with activities of intrinsic value.

PRESIDENT COLE: That is right. We have to find ways to give prestige and status to these activities to the point that they can subvert the peer culture and bring about a revolution within it.

B. J. BORRESON (*Executive Dean for Student Life, University of Maryland*): Dr. Gross, I am interested that most of your illustrations exclude the classroom. Those of us who are actually responsible for the orientation programs are faced with the fact that the students are going to end up in English I, Mathematics I, Biology I, and whatever other courses they have to take. To put it in the student vernacular, we get them all "jazzed up" about the love of learning for its own sake; then we submit them to an environment the spirit of which, in the first year at least, is quite contrary to this. In most colleges, I think, these initial experiences develop a kind of schizophrenia with which we are not prepared to deal.

The experiences most freshmen have after the usual "pep talks" are very different from the ones we are talking about here. For example, the kind of teacher who can draw applause from five hundred students is a very rare bird, indeed. I think we have to face the fact that we often create expectations that we can't fulfill. This is why seniors are often cynics.

DR. GROSS: Well, I think I am going to have to take refuge in the remark Plato made when he was asked how on earth his ideal state would ever come about. He replied that this was not his responsibility, that all he had to do was describe it. One doesn't criticize a sculptor for producing a beautiful figure, even though it may never otherwise exist.

I still think we have to know what we are trying to do, and I don't think that what I have suggested here has anything to do with any particular time or place. Maybe we are out of joint right now, but that doesn't mean that we should turn away from our goal. You weren't suggesting that.

DEAN BORRESON: No, quite the contrary. I was simply saying that I think the dominant emphasis in the modern American university, especially in the classroom, is directly opposite to what you are describing as the ideal.

DR. GROSS: I think that is an overstatement. I believe many teachers of freshman English or mathematics are trying to achieve the very objectives we have been talking about, and I believe they deserve encouragement from other quarters.

EUGENE S. WILSON (*Dean of Admission, Amherst College*): Dean Borreson has raised a point that this group could profitably discuss for the next day and a half, namely, the overexpectation of freshmen. Our handbooks and picture-books mention our Nobel prize winners and great scholars, and they show happy students close to happy teachers. We paint a glowing picture of the excitement of learning in our orientation programs; then we send the freshmen into classes they find dull and routine. Our orientation programs have failed because we have said, "This is the excitement of learning," and the students' experience has said, "These are the realities."

I was chatting with a senior from a well-known university the other day, and I asked him about his experience in his freshman and sophomore years. He said, "It was simply horrible. I had the worst teachers I ever had. Half of my teachers were graduate students who didn't give a damn about me, but I didn't expect anything different in the first two years so it didn't trouble me."

Maybe successful orientation consists in making expectations realistic and in explaining to freshmen exactly what is in store for them. Coming from high schools where things were made simple for them, they may not consider a teacher good if he asks them to act differently.

PRESIDENT COLE: The assumption always seems to be that we should subject the freshmen and sophomores to large lecture classes and reserve the small seminars for the juniors and seniors so that students will have more contact with faculty members as their work becomes more intense. I wonder if this whole system isn't upside down. Ideally, the faculty ought gradually to go out of business. A successful teacher makes himself less and less necessary to the student.

If a student has had good teaching and close association with his professors during the first two years, he can survive in large classes his last two years, for by that time he has learned to work independently. Isn't it a mistake, therefore, to make budgetary savings at the expense of freshmen and sophomores for the benefit of juniors and seniors? Shouldn't it be the other way around?

DR. GROSS: Large lecture classes are not created at the expense of freshmen. Only the best professors can teach them. If anyone else is drafted, the institution is not doing its job responsibly. If good teachers are enlisted, I don't see anything bad about it. Freshmen get really first-class teaching. I think we actually improved history teaching when we changed from sections of 45 students to large lecture groups of 350. Furthermore, I don't think it is mechanically possible to invert this system. There are not enough students in advanced courses to make up large classes; moreover, advanced courses are less likely to lend themselves to this type of teaching.

JOHN R. HILLS (*Director, Testing and Guidance, Regents of the University System of Georgia*): One thing that caught my attention in your address this evening was your comment to the effect that beautiful buildings and attractive grounds contribute beneficially to the climate of learning. Where I come from, we are getting along with functional buildings, and we are not developing especially attractive grounds like Princeton's. It hadn't occurred to me that this might be a step in the wrong direction. Are physical surroundings really critical or relevant?

DR. GROSS: I have a feeling that we ought to do any single thing we can in the four years to enrich the esthetic aspects of the student's life. What we do will vary with the locality. If one happens to live in Santa Barbara and doesn't take advantage of the shore line, he is just a dope.

Within reasonable financial limits, we ought to do whatever we can to make life rich and exciting. We can do it in an urban university in one way and in a country college in another way. The point is that we should use every device at our disposal, whether it is architectural or horticultural, to provide as full an experience as we can. I don't think a single bit of this effort is wasted.

At Rutgers, we have just started this year something we should have started years ago. We open the chapel at noon and have the organist play for a half or three-quarters of an hour. It is amazing how many students drop in. This is music, not flowers, but the idea is the same: it adds to the enrichment of the human spirit.

I think we sometimes have to remind ourselves that we do not have brains alone, or bodies alone, on our campus. We have people, with all their manifold interests, and certain opportunities for touching them. We never know when we will hit a particular person where he lives, so we should use every resource we have.

RECENT RESEARCH ON
THE AMERICAN COLLEGE STUDENT: 1

NEVITT SANFORD
Professor of Psychology,
University of California, Berkeley

W E MIGHT begin discussing the introduction of entering students to the intellectual life of the college by asking ourselves what the entering freshman is like and by using recent research to provide a general description of him. We must remember, however, that research is not just a matter of collecting data and turning on the machines. We have a right and an obligation to think about the data we collect. With this obligation in mind, consider this description of the typical freshman entering Vassar College:

The typical freshman begins her life with eagerness and confidence. She is proud to be a member of the college community and wants to live up to the honor of having been admitted. Knowing pretty well what the next few years hold for her, she is relatively untroubled by questions of what to do or be. She is oriented primarily to the social group, and her very considerable social skill is freely displayed. She is friendly, co-operative, polite, and, at least in her external aspect, poised. She accepts uncritically the values of her family and her home community, has high respect for social institutions, and she is deferential and uncomplaining toward the powers-that-be. This last attitude extends even to psychological testers. She approaches her tests on the first day of school with eager compliance. The crowded auditorium in which she labors for two hours is sensationally quiet. And, joy to the researcher, all the test items are completed.[1]

In sum, the typical Vassar freshman is idealistic, sociable, well organized, and well behaved. Small wonder that on the standard-

---

[1] N. Sanford, "The Uncertain Senior," *Journal of the National Association of Women Deans and Counselors,* XXI (1957), 9–15.

ized personality tests she scores as a pretty sound and healthy specimen. But this stable freshman is in for some eye-opening, disillusioning, broadening, and maturing experiences. Midway through her senior year, the chances are that she will feel rather confused, frustrated, and anxious; she will look back on her freshman year as a remote and happy time.

How shall we explain this pattern of behavior on the part of the freshman? Let me suggest several ways in which we have to look at the freshman. First, we have to understand in what ways the freshman is like everybody else. Second, we have to consider the qualities that each freshman shares with some freshmen but not with others, that is to say, individual differences. Third, we have to note the characteristics that distinguish a freshman from older and younger people. Finally, we have to see what distinguishes him from those in the same age group who don't go on to college.

In considering the freshman as a human being, it is well to remember that underneath the rather smooth exterior he is probably just as confused and complicated as the rest of us. We should remember also that the principles of personality development hold true for the freshman in the same way they do for other people. If we bear in mind that personality development moves toward higher levels of complexity, that is to say, higher levels of differentiation and integration, then we can understand that the freshman, like other people, moves toward greater freedom of impulse, greater enlightenment of conscience, and greater consciousness in shaping his own personality. The freshman can do this, but this does not distinguish him from anybody else. Everybody can move in these directions if the necessary conditions are present. Like everybody else, the freshman also resists changes. He has already developed a personality structure that he thinks and hopes will suffice for the challenges that are to come; hence, it is up to the college to confront him with some challenges that he cannot handle without evolving new responses.

Just as there are profound human resemblances, there are also marked individual differences. One might even say that all persons are alike in that each one is different. Individual differences have been vividly described by McConnell and his associates at the Center for the Study of Higher Education at Berkeley.[2] We know from their work that there is enormous diversity among entering freshmen, diversity among colleges, and diversity among students entering any particular college. The range of scores is very wide with respect to any characteristic that might possibly interest us. The implications of this diversity for the problem we are discussing today are clear. If the intellectual abilities of all the students entering one institution are below the average of students entering another institution, then the problem of introducing these two groups of students to the intellectual life of the college is bound to be different in the two cases.

So it is with respect to values. If at one institution the students hold very high theoretical and esthetic values and are relatively unconventional, the task of introducing them to the intellectual life of the college is very different from what it is at a college where the students yearn primarily for social status and glamour. I shall not dwell on these differences because we have Dr. Goldsen[3] and others here who have done much of the research in this area. I should mention in this connection, however, the kinds of differences reported by Elizabeth Douvan and her associates at the Survey Research Center of the University of Michigan.[4] Based on national samples of boy scouts and girl scouts in high school, these studies show great variation in the motives boys and girls have in going to college. In general, boys think of college in terms of their vocational interests, while girls tend to think of college in terms of glamour and romance. I might add here that I am not referring to the "romance of learning" about which President Gross spoke last night. As all of you know, some college girls pursue learning while others learn pursuing. The difference is striking!

Another very interesting and important difference, according to

[2] T. R. McConnell and P. Heist, "Do Students Make the College?" *College and University,* XXXV (1959), 442–52; also "The Diverse College Student Population," in *The American College,* ed. Nevitt Sanford (New York: Wiley, 1961).

[3] R. Goldsen *et al., What College Students Think* (Princeton, N.J.: D. Van Nostrand Co., 1960).

[4] E. Douvan and C. Kaye, "Motivational Factors in College Entrance," in Sanford (ed.) , *op. cit.*

Douvan,[5] is that boys arrive much earlier than girls at the crisis in respect to independence or autonomy. When they arrive at college, boys have already been through a struggle for independence from their parents and strive very hard to maintain that independence. On the other hand, girls in the same age range and at the same place are much more submissive than boys to parents and other adults. Accordingly, we can expect girls to be more responsive to the efforts of teachers to introduce them into the intellectual life of the college. They will be very agreeable, deferential, compliant —like the Vassar girls described earlier. The question is: Will what we do at this time have lasting effects? The evidence is that many girls reach the crisis in establishing independence about the time they leave college. When girls like those who go to Vassar think about setting up an apartment in New York and getting a job, they face the same kind of problem respecting independence from parents that boys typically face at about the time they are entering college.

Let us now consider the freshman as a late adolescent and the ways in which he differs from older and younger people. Among other things, the growth curves based on the test scores of people of various ages show some significant differences. For example, the curves based on measures of intellectual ability show the freshman is somewhere between the high school sophomore and the college senior in respect to a wide variety of intellectual traits. With respect to personality tests, however, there is not much that we can point to. It is very difficult to devise personality tests that are valid for people in widely different age ranges. An example of the few age differences in personality that have been demonstrated is provided by the scores on the Strong Interest Blank. These show some curves extending from the age of nine or ten to adulthood. I remember Strong's reporting some years ago that, as boys grow older, their interests become more feminine and that, as girls grow up, their interests become more masculine.[6] The relationship with age is complicated by the fact that the masculinity-femininity of

[5] Douvan, "Independence and Identity in Adolescents," *Children,* IV (1957), 186–90.
[6] E. K. Strong, *Vocational Interests of Men and Women* (Stanford, Calif.: Stanford University Press, 1943).

interests also correlates with education. In any case, it seems reasonable that, as boys finally establish their masculinity in a more or less comfortable way, they are less compelled to emphasize masculinity in the expression of their interests. This is an age-linked factor that helps to distinguish the late adolescent from other people.

A set of test scores does not go very far, however, toward describing the personality of the freshman. What we need is a way of describing him that shows the relationships among the various attributes of his personality, a way that depicts him as a whole personality and, particularly, as a personality in a stage of development.

When we say "stage of development," we must have in mind a conception of a *course* of development, development toward something. I have suggested that it is toward greater complexity of the personality. We must also have a notion of the progressive nature of change, an appreciation of the fact that things proceed in some kind of order, that certain things have to be accomplished before certain other things are possible, and that the occurrence of certain events creates a kind of readiness that makes it possible for external stimuli to induce actual changes in the personality.

Where does the freshman or the seventeen- or eighteen-year-old stand in this course of development? It is possible to describe a stage of development that we can call late adolescence. It is marked by a kind of premature adulthood. It seems to me that the freshman is like a convert to adulthood; that is to say, he overdoes the controlling aspect of his personality. We might say that he is in a stage of having just mastered to some degree his impulse life; he is just over the storm and stress of adolescence. The battle has been won, or at least there has been a retreat to prepared positions, so that the freshman is like the Vassar girl I described—organized, controlled, and conventional. But this condition, I suggest, is fairly tenuous. There is an exaggeration of moral strictness, of striving for purity and perfection. This is because the controlling mechanisms are rather new; the individual is not quite used to them yet and is not able to use them in a flexible way. Thus, we might say that the entering freshman is in an authoritarian stage.

The freshman is pretty strict in his moral requirements upon himself and others. This idealism of the freshman is partly caused by the necessity for being very, very different from what he was just a little while ago, when he felt more or less overwhelmed by his impulses. One of the good sides of this is the freshman's intolerance of anything hypocritical or phony. He wants a clear-cut and unambiguous picture of his hero, and he is not prepared for the discovery that his heroes have feet of clay. This is one aspect of his somewhat stereotyped thinking, the tendency to see things in blacks and whites, which is more characteristic of the freshman than of older students.

Another aspect of the authoritarian stage is the need for external support for the moral positions that have been taken. This we see very clearly in the freshman. As I suggested, he is still under the sway of family and community standards, but he can remain so only if he has external support for his system of values. It is this state of affairs that is responsible for the freshman's susceptibility to influence either by the adult authorities of the college or by the student peer group. Since the freshman usually does not get much attention from adults, he typically seeks support for his conventional moral position from the college peer culture. The freshman's whole structure of dispositions and values is somewhat rigid. Sooner or later, it has to give way to educational challenges so that a more differentiated and flexible structure can develop.

I want to mention also the special position of the entering freshman with respect to self-esteem. The Vassar girl whom I described appears to think that she is really quite all right. After all, she has the label of "all rightness" upon her because she has been admitted to the college and has been told by various people that she is among the select few. She may very well believe that all she has to do is to go on being the person she is in order to continue getting the kinds of rewards that she has recently received.

So, in contrast to the senior, this freshman is relatively untroubled about herself, at least on the surface. In a general way, she knows what her next four years hold for her. Most important decisions can be postponed. But all the great decisions of life are still ahead of the freshman, and she knows this. The question of vocation, the question about relations with the opposite sex, the question about the kinds of values she is ultimately going to have

—all these are still ahead; consequently, it doesn't take very much to upset the freshman's sense of confidence and self-esteem. The very first failure will, in many cases, be quite upsetting. I am assuming that there are bound to be failures; moreover, I am assuming that some failures, if they are not too traumatic, are all to the good because they are stimuli for further growth.

In his uncertainty about himself, the freshman shows a tendency to overestimate what he is and what he can do, together with a tendency to fall into very serious underestimation of himself. He wavers back and forth from an exaggerated belief in his powers to depression, withdrawal, and an unwillingness to try. One way out of this uncertainty, frequently chosen by boys particularly, is an early declaration of what his professional role is going to be. David Beardslee and Donald O'Dowd[7] have shown that among college students and faculties there is a clear conception of the prestige hierarchy of the professions and that as soon as a person says he is going into a given profession, he begins to be regarded by his fellows in the same way that people already in that profession are regarded. So, if a freshman wants to be quite clear about himself and to feel that he is all right and that he knows where he is going, all he has to do is to say he is going into one of the high-level professions; then he has identified himself to his colleagues, who begin to react to him as if he were already a scientist, a doctor, or a lawyer. The trouble with this mode of adaptation is not only that the student often makes false or inappropriate choices but also that it often causes a premature closure of the personality and seriously interferes with the kind of development that we like to see.

Then there is the question of what distinguishes the freshman from people in his age range who do not go to college. If there were time, this would be the place to describe the work of Havighurst,[8] Wise,[9] and Douvan.[10] Leaving home is an extremely important event. The major external supports for the young per-

[7] Beardslee and O'Dowd, "Students and the Occupational World," in Sanford (ed.), *op. cit.*

[8] R. J. Havighurst, *American Higher Education in the 1960's* (Columbus: Ohio State University Press, 1960).

[9] W. Max Wise, *They Come for the Best of Reasons—College Students Today* (Washington: American Council on Education, 1958).

[10] Douvan, *op. cit.*

son's way of looking at the world and adapting to it are suddenly withdrawn, and he has to evolve inner supports or else find external substitutes for the parental authority. Most freshmen do the latter. Another crucial aspect of the freshman's situation arises from the fact that he is now confronted with problems and tasks that are going to test him in a way that he hasn't been tested before. He hopes that he can meet these tests by being the same person that he has been, but he cannot, of course, remain the same.

Let me now mention some implications of research for the problem that we are here to discuss. It has already been pointed out that the major forces that oppose us when we try to initiate the freshman into the intellectual life are the student peer culture, which makes relatively few or no intellectual demands, and an adult culture, which accents grades or the practical aspects of college experience.

It follows from what I have said that if the faculty is ever going to have close and influential relationships with students, these relationships must be established at the beginning of the freshman year. The main purpose of the freshman year in any college should be to win the freshman to the intellectual life. In most cases, this cannot possibly be done except by the faculty. I believe that the faculty has a great opportunity at this point because the freshman is wide open to influence by adults. If arrangements can be made for the faculty members to become important figures in the lives of the students, this might very well turn the trick for many who now are lost to the intellectual enterprise.

I would like to urge, also, that we tell the freshman the truth about the college. This means letting him in on the knowledge we have about what things are really like in the college and the knowledge we have about what students are like. I see no reason at all why a freshman cannot be given a better idea of what he can expect. Above all, it seems to me, he must be confronted with the idea that he is supposed to change and, indeed, with the idea that this should be his main *purpose* in college. He is not in college to go on being the same person he has been in the past. The whole point of college is to get the freshman to change and to help him acquire new adaptive devices for becoming a different and better person.

RECENT RESEARCH ON THE AMERICAN COLLEGE STUDENT: 2

ROSE K. GOLDSEN
Associate Professor,
Department of Sociology and Anthropology,
Cornell University

SINCE THIS conference is concerned with the introduction of entering students to the intellectual life of the college, I have culled the research which my colleagues and I have been conducting during the decade of the fifties[1] and have selected some findings that I think are relevant to this problem. I have also summarized some major trends that seem to me to indicate intellectual development.

Let me tell you the names of the colleges and universities we studied: Cornell, Dartmouth, Fisk, Harvard, Michigan, North Carolina, Texas, University of California at Los Angeles, Wayne, Wesleyan, and Yale. This is certainly not a national sample, but it is a good selection of influential universities throughout the country, and it includes widely different types, for example, Harvard and Wayne.

I have selected five indications of "intellectual outlook" to discuss here, and I shall list them briefly:

1. The belief that basic education and appreciation of ideas should be a principal aim of college education.

2. The belief that occupational life should serve noninstrumental values of creativity and service.

3. Religious belief that is not principally authoritarianism and dogma.

---

[1] R. K. Goldsen, M. Rosenberg, R. M. Williams, Jr., and E. A. Suchman, *What College Students Think* (Princeton, N.J.: D. Van Nostrand Co., 1960).

4. Tolerance of another's right to hold a deviant, unorthodox, even unpopular position.

5. Differentiated rather than monolithic beliefs and attitudes in political and economic matters. (The opposite of this is an ism.)

BASIC EDUCATION AND APPRECIATION OF IDEAS

What do students at these institutions think are the main purposes of a college education? What do they think college is all about? In general, the evidence indicates that, as the students go through college, values which I would define as intellectual are the ones that are most encouraged and reinforced. For example, the principle that a broad general education is important for its own sake is such a value, and more students are won over to this point of view than to any other.

The students we studied evaluate their college education by applying several sets of standards simultaneously. They believe that the college ought to stress many things: basic education and the appreciation of ideas, one's ability to get along with different kinds of people, preparation for a career, knowledge of and interest in community and world problems, moral and ethical standards and values. All these—and more—are considered by the majority of the students we polled to be highly important educational values deserving emphasis in college. When they are pinned down, however, these students hold three fairly clear "philosophies" above all others: an academic philosophy (that a basic education and the appreciation of ideas are important in and of themselves); a vocational philosophy (that vocational training and skills are necessary for effectiveness in one's career); and an interpersonal philosophy (that the ability to get along with different people contributes to a satisfying life). Only occasionally do we encounter students who do not consider these aims central to college education.

Let us now picture the freshmen entering college at the broad end of a funnel and the seniors emerging at the narrow end. What happens inside the funnel? On the campuses we studied, support for "basic education" is reinforced and encouraged more than that for any of the other philosophies. Belief in the value of basic education and appreciation of ideas not only holds those who entered college with this view of its main purpose, but also gains the most new recruits.[2] Students who start out with this point of view are most likely to maintain it; students who start out with any other point of view are very likely to be won over to the idea of education for its own sake. This is true even of students in professional curricula, such as engineering.

The point to be emphasized here is that these campuses "social-ize" the students to acknowledge the legitimacy of broad general education for its own sake. The campus milieu implicitly educates many students to view education as desirable for its own sake and to view as most desirable the kind of education that stresses this principle.

CREATIVITY AND SERVICE IN OCCUPATIONAL LIFE

What about the meaning of work? The evidence shows that the college students we studied tend to develop an approach to their work that I would define as intellectual. This is to say, freshmen are more inclined to stress "what work can do for me"; seniors, "what I can do with my work."

College students expect their work and career to be more than simply a way to earn a living. When they mention the principal value they expect their work to serve, they again apply several sets of standards simultaneously. Work should, they tell us, provide an opportunity for creativity; it should be of help to others; it should allow one to work with people; it should provide security and in-come as well as a certain amount of status and prestige. In addi-tion, work should offer opportunities for leadership and adven-ture and give free play to one's abilities, aptitudes, and training. All these things are considered highly important by substantial proportions of the students we studied.

Some of these values I have listed are instrumental in the sense that they stress "what work will do for me"; others are goal values in that they stress "what I can do with my work." Security and

---

[2] Statements concerning changes in students' beliefs and attitudes are based on two types of evidence. First, a comparison was made of the testimony given by freshmen, sophomores, juniors, and seniors at eleven universities. Such a comparison supports only an inference about change. These inferences were checked by examining panel interviews with 944 Cornell students who had been interviewed as underclassmen and as upperclassmen. (This was the only university supplying such developmental data.)

money are associated with the first; creativity and service, with the second. The important finding is that among the entering students it was an instrumental value—security—that was most widely appealing; a goal value—creativity—that lagged behind. Yet, among seniors the order had shifted. Among seniors the appeal of creativity was more widespread, and the appeal of security lagged noticeably behind.

RELATIVISTIC CONCEPTION OF THE DEITY

What about religion? Again, the evidence shows that during the college years the students tend to develop an approach that I would label "intellectual." That is to say, cant, orthodoxy, and rigid interpretations of God and religion are not encouraged, whereas relativism and broad personal beliefs about God and religion are reinforced and adopted by many. The tendency, therefore, is to move away from orthodoxy—not away from belief, but away from orthodoxy.

To illustrate this change in approach, let me cite their changing conception of the Deity. There are three clearly discernible viewpoints among the students we studied: (a) the viewpoint that God is a personified Divine Being with very specific attributes; (b) the viewpoint that He is, rather, a general and mysterious Power whose attributes are open to individual interpretation; and (c) a decidedly minority viewpoint—however expressed and whatever it may mean—that avoids terms such as God, Divine, and Being and refers instead to Humanity, Natural Law, and the like.

Now, among beginning students it is the first view of the Deity that is most widespread; among seniors it is the second. The evidence shows that it is not disbelief or unbelief that develops during the college years; on the contrary, it is a relativistic view of the Deity that develops, gaining its new recruits not from the orthodox but from the wavering believers and unbelievers.

The orthodox view of the Deity is the staunchest one. Students are not easily shaken loose from it. On the other hand, very few are won over to this view during college. Likewise, few deflect from a belief in a personal, relativistic God, and this is the only viewpoint that gains more supporters than it loses. This is the kind of belief, in short, that is encouraged during the college years. Let me say again that we have found no evidence that during college unbelief or disbelief is reinforced. If religious belief is modified in any way during these years, uncertainty, deviant belief, and unbelief tend to become relativistic belief.

TOLERANCE OF RIGHT TO HOLD DEVIANT VIEWPOINTS

How about tolerance toward special groups and "unpopular" ideas? To cite just one example, students' attitudes toward conscientious objectors become more tolerant in college. I mention this particular attitude because it is an especially good barometer of one's willingness to respect another's right to hold a deviant, unorthodox position. We have no easily recognized "good" and "bad" rhetoric on this subject as we have, say, on racial attitudes.

Our study included a series of items that formed a scale of attitudes toward conscientious objectors. On two of the items in this scale there was a 30 percent shift in two years in the climate of opinion toward increased tolerance for conscientious objectors. Many of the students we studied had evidently learned to respect another person's right to act on his own conviction, however deviant or unpopular.

DIFFERENTIATED VIEWPOINT IN SOCIAL AND ECONOMIC MATTERS

What about political and economic beliefs? We find evidence that during the college years the students' political and economic beliefs become differentiated rather than stereotypic or monolithic—another indicator, as I see it, of a healthy intellectual development.

We know that in the decade of the fifties the trend on most campuses was toward increased conservatism in political and economic beliefs. Which is more indicative of a healthy intellectual climate, conservatism or liberalism? Of course, the question posed in this way is unanswerable. What is there about political and economic beliefs, then, that can be considered a useful indication of healthy intellectual development?

I submit that if we find political and economic beliefs differentiated and varied rather than stereotypic and opinionated, we have an indication of healthy intellectual development. If we find

down-the-line conservatism or liberalism no matter what the issues are, we are likely to be dealing with dogma.

Our data show that differentiation of beliefs is likely to occur
during the college years. Down-the-line condemnation by conservative students of all stands usually considered liberal diminishes
as freshmen move along. I have time to cite only one example. In
contrast to the freshmen, seniors who uphold a conservative (that
is, laissez faire) economic philosophy are just as likely as others to
support "government interference" in behalf of humanitarian
causes (for example, provision of widespread free college education).

Other Factors Influencing Intellectual Outlook

So far, I have spoken only of broad, general trends showing
shifts in opinion that I would call evidence of intellectual development. Now let us look at the other side of the coin. Nothing I
have said here can be taken as justification for complacency. I
have spoken about net gains. I have made "more so" or "less so"
statements. I have not mentioned the vast subgroups of the college
population who are untouched by the intellectual trends I have
chosen to talk about. These subgroups form what we call "insulat-
ing subsystems," which slow up or inhibit the kinds of changes I
have been discussing. Fraternities constitute such a subsystem on
certain campuses. Curricula and course specialization often create
subsystems of the same type. No trend I have mentioned is pervasive enough or sweeping enough to justify a feeling of content-
ment about the job our colleges are doing in promoting the intellectual development of our students.

Although we must always keep this caveat in mind, we must not
lose sight of the fact that there is a net gain. On the basis of present evidence, we can confidently say that more seniors than freshmen uphold intellectual values and take an intellectual approach
to serious problems. The findings of research call attention to
what is almost a sociological truism and yet is often overlooked:
if young people are exposed to a social environment for four
years, they will become socialized to the dominant values of that
environment and will acknowledge their legitimacy.

The college and university campus constitutes one of the very few places in American culture where intellectual values are explicit and carry authoritative weight. The socialization process lends its weight to the reinforcement of these values. No matter what counterthemes there are (and there *are* counterthemes), respect for intellectual values "rubs off" on the students. The burden is on the colleges to keep these intellectual values alive, vigorous, and effective. The students catch on.

How are we to measure the success of our colleges and universities in conveying intellectual values? Many a senior tells us, "This is the way I see it now, but if only I had known from the beginning what I know now, I'd have gone through college quite differently. I feel that my first two or three years were a waste of time." If the senior says this, is he telling us that we have failed or that we have succeeded?

Is the senior attesting to the success of college education or to its failure? I leave the question open.

RECENT RESEARCH ON INSTITUTIONAL CLIMATES: 1

Continuity and Contrast in the Transition from High School to College

GEORGE G. STERN
Professor of Psychology,
Syracuse University

T HE ISSUES of this conference remind me of a story from Israel a few years ago, describing the difference between an optimist and a pessimist. After contemplating the problems facing Israel at that time, an optimistic Israeli said, "The thing for us to do is to declare war on the United States. They will send a task force over here and leave all sorts of equipment. By the time they are done with us, all of our economic problems will be solved." The pessimist's reply was, "But what if we should win?"

The irony of the story is reflected in the position in which we now seem to find ourselves. The optimists appear to be saying that students come to us unmotivated, apathetic, anti-intellectual, and overconforming. Although the optimist knows that all of these attributes create very, very difficult problems for us in educating college students, he has the notion that American know-how will see us through again, that someone will find a technique for increasing the motivation of students. In this context, the pessimist seems to say, "But what if they should come to college *to learn?*"

Current studies of the high school peer culture (Brookover;[1] Coleman;[2] Gordon[3]) make it clear that academic achievement is

[1] W. B. Brookover, "The Social Roles of Teachers and Pupil Achievement," *American Sociological Review*, VIII (1943), 389–93.

[2] J. S. Coleman, "Academic Achievement and the Structure of Competition," *Har-*

a poor source of status or prestige among teen-agers. Students might be expected to carry these same values with them into college, at least to the extent of believing that high grades would not be held against an outstanding student provided he had made no effort to earn them. Although this might seem consistent with the tendency toward apathy, privatism, and indifference so widely remarked on today (Cole, Derber, and Gans;[4] Jacob[5]), several observers have been struck by the high level of expectancy that students at a number of schools have for college as a learning experience (Eddy;[6] Sussmann[7]). Superficially, it would appear difficult to reconcile these two sets of observations.

Our knowledge of the transition from high school to college has been limited in the past to attempts to predict college grades from high school performance. It has been only in the last two or three years that a body of literature dealing with high school and college as social processes has begun to emerge (Herriott and Trask;[8] Fishman[9]). The study to be described here shows this same orientation and is concerned specifically with the contrast between student appraisals of their high school as learning environments, the expectations they bring to college, and their descriptions as college seniors of the experience they have had.

An Approach to the Study of Psychological Characteristics of Learning Environments

The psychological environment may be thought of as a complex of stimuli that press upon the individual and to which his behav-

[3] C. W. Gordon, *The Social System of the High School: A Study in the Sociology of Adolescence* (Glencoe, Ill.: Free Press, 1957).

[4] C. C. Cole, Jr., M. Derber, and C. B. Gans, "How Can a Campus Climate Be Created, for Favorable Development of Quality Programs, by Involving the Participation of Faculty, Students, and Administrators?" in *Current Issues in Higher Education, 1960*, ed. G. K. Smith (Washington: Association for Higher Education, 1960), pp. 132–37.

[5] P. E. Jacob, *Changing Values in College* (New York: Harper & Bros., 1957).

[6] E. D. Eddy, Jr., *The College Influence on Student Character* (Washington: American Council on Education, 1959).

[7] C. Sussmann, *Freshman Morale at M.I.T.* (Cambridge: Massachusetts Institute of Technology, 1960).

[8] R. E. Herriott and A. E. Trask (eds.), "Theory and Research in Sociology and Education," *Harvard Educational Review*, A Special Issue; XXIX (1959), 275–404.

[9] J. A. Fishman (ed.), "The Social Psychology of School-to-College Transition," *Journal of Educational Sociology*, Special Issue, XXXIII (1960), 249–304.

ior constitutes a response. In a sense, these pressures are unique and private insofar as the view that each of us has of the world must be ultimately and inevitably private. As observers, however, we tend to draw conclusions of our own regarding the meaning of the events in which someone else is participating, and we also tend to organize and classify otherwise discrete events on the basis of seemingly common elements. In an academic setting, for example, there may be several alternative implications to the fact that resident students at a given college must get written permission to be away from college overnight. If we also observe, however, that students are often kept waiting when they have appointments with faculty members, that freshmen have to take orders from upperclassmen for a period of time, and that the school administration will not tolerate student complaints or protests, we may feel justified in inferring that there is a strong pressure toward the development of responses involving student *abasement* at this school.

Some years ago, Murray[10] introduced a taxonomy for classifying both the environmental pressures and the characteristic ways in which an individual strives to structure the environment for himself. He called the external pressures *press,* their internal counterparts *needs.* Both needs and press are inferred from characteristic activities and events, the former from things that the individual typically does, the latter from things that are typically done to him in some particular setting. Students with high needs for *abasement,* for example, might perhaps regard a school with a strong press for abasement as especially congenial. The strength of an abasement need could be judged by the extent to which the student appears to enjoy taking the blame for something done by his friends, likes telling others about his mistakes and failures, tries to figure out how he was to blame whenever he is involved in an argument, and dislikes making a fuss when someone deliberately takes advantage of him.

The measurement of needs and press

The Activities Index and College Characteristics Index are questionnaries developed respectively for the measurement of

[10] H. A. Murray, *Explorations in Personality: A Clinical and Experimental Study of Fifty Men of College Age* (New York: Oxford University Press, 1938).

needs and press (Stern[11]). The Activities Index was developed originally in collaboration with B. S. Bloom, M. I. Stein, and H. Lane[12] for use in the Chicago studies of student personality assessment (Stern, Stein, and Bloom[13]). It consists of 300 items describing commonplace daily activities similar to those used as illustrations of need abasement above, distributed among 30 scales of ten items, to each of which the individual records his like or dislike.

The College Characteristics Index, developed in collaboration with C. R. Pace,[14] has a design similar to that of the Activities Index. The items, however, describe activities, policies, procedures, attitudes, and impressions that might be characteristic of various types of undergraduate college settings. The indexes have been employed in an extensive study of American colleges sponsored by the U.S. Office of Education and reported in part elsewhere by Pace[15] and by Stern,[16] as well as in a related investigation by Thistlethwaite.[17]

A High School Characteristics Index has recently been prepared with the aid of J. Dopyera, V. L. Woolston, E. K. Woolfolk, and J. Lyons, and an adaption for use in evening colleges has been completed by C. Winters, S. Archer, and D. Meyer.

---

[11] G. G. Stern, *Preliminary Manual: Activities Index; College Characteristics Index* (Syracuse, N.Y.: Psychological Research Center, Syracuse University Research Institute, 1958).

[12] With the assistance of James Abegglen, Paul Baer, Sharon Goldberg, James Sachs, Mary McCord Tyler, and Dorothy Whitman. Subsequent revisions have been contributed to by Fred Carleton, Louis DiAngelo, John Scanlon, Walter Stellwagen, Charles Van Buskirk, and others.

[13] G. G. Stern, M. I. Stein, and B. S. Bloom, *Methods in Personality Assessment* (Glencoe, Ill.: Free Press, 1956).

[14] C. R. Pace and G. G. Stern, "An Approach to the Measurement of Psychological Characteristics of College Environments," *Journal of Educational Psychology*, XLIX (1958), 269–77. (The index was developed with the assistance of Barnett Denton, Sally Donovan, Harriet Dorn, Eugene Farber, Dagny Henderson, Anne McFee, and others.)

[15] Pace, "Five College Environments," *College Board Review*, Spring 1960, pp. 24–28.

[16] Stern, "Congruence and Dissonance in the Ecology of College Students," *Student Medicine*, VIII (1960), 304–39; "Student Values and Their Relationship to the College Environment," in *Research on College Students*, ed. H. T. Sprague (Boulder, Colo.: Western Interstate Commission for Higher Education, 1960); "The Measurement of Psychological Characteristics of Learning Environments," in *Personality Measurement*, eds. S. J. Messick and J. Ross (New York: Wiley, in press); "Environments for Learning," in *The American College: A Psychological and Social Interpretation of the Higher Learning*, ed. R. N. Sanford (New York: Wiley, 1961).

[17] D. C. Thistlethwaite, "College Environments and the Development of Talent," *Science*, CXXX (1959), 71–76; "College Press and Student Achievement," *Journal of Educational Psychology*, L (1959), 183–91.

A Study of High School and College Press

During freshman orientation week the incoming class of over 2,000 entrants at a major Eastern university were given the High School Characteristics Index, with instructions to fill this out in relation to the high school from which they graduated, and the College Characteristics Index, to be responded to in terms of the expectations they had regarding the university which they were now entering. The following four subgroups were pulled from the total class:

Private preparatory: 103 entrants from 63 different schools

Parochial: 89 entrants from 42 different schools

Local public: 96 entrants from a local public high school, the largest single source for this university, and consisting coincidentally of students essentially comparable in socioeconomic class level with those from the private preparatory schools

Nonlocal public: 29 entrants from a distant metropolitan high school also comparable in socioeconomic class level with the private preparatory schools

Also available for analysis were College Characteristics Index data describing this university, which had been obtained from 1,036 graduating seniors in the preceeding spring of the same year (Stern[18]).

Results

The presentation of findings based on the thirty scales from each of these instruments is facilitated by the fact that a systematic pattern of interrelationships has been found to hold for these scales. The nature of these relationships is shown in Figure 1, in which each wedge corresponds to a scale. Adjacent wedges represent scales which are highly correlated; uncorrelated scales have been laid out 90° apart from one another, and negatively correlated scales are on opposite sides of the circle.

Professor Fred Hauck of the Syracuse University School of Art is responsible for the graphic figures superimposed on the chart in Figure 1, which help dramatize the essential elements in the internal structure of these scales. The combination of scales in the lower left portion of the circle suggests peculiarly intrapersonal

[18] Stern, "Student Values and Their Relationship to the College Environment," in *Research on College Students.*

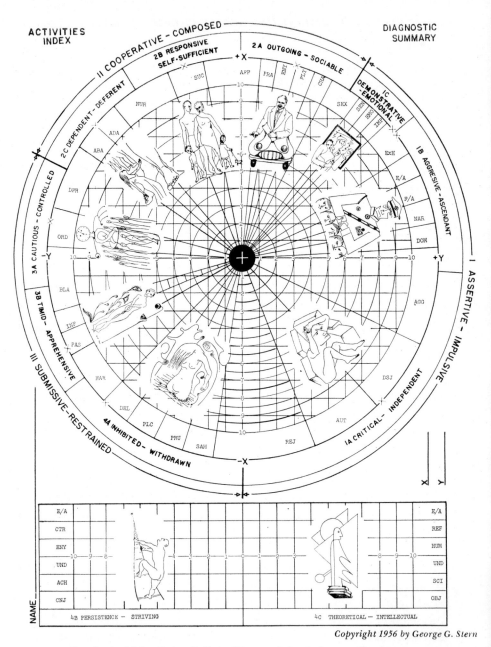

FIG. 1.—Activities Index–College Characteristics Index profile structure.

and depressed activities, which give way to increasingly sociable patterns of behavior toward the top and become increasingly outgoing and assertive toward the right.

It will be sufficient for our present purposes to note three major axes of this chart, as yielded by a second-order factoring of the scales. A diagonal from lower left to upper right across the circle would coincide with *emotional control* and *expression*. A second diagonal from upper left to lower right may be described in terms of *dependency pressures* versus *autonomy*. The third dimension is embodied in the grid at the bottom of the chart and is concerned exclusively with characteristics of the *intellectual orientation*.

As shown in Figure 2, actual scale scores are entered on each wedge from zero at the center to a maximum of ten at the periphery. The one on the left suggests a distant, self-assertive individual with fantasies of personal achievement and intellectual precocity. The faculty noted independently that this student was antagonistic, individualistic, and dreamlike, with a suggested capacity for work that he never fulfilled. The profile to the right is at the opposite extreme in suggesting a person characterized by emotional withdrawal, depressed affect, lowered self-esteem, minimal drive level, and modest intellectual characteristics. This student was an early withdrawal who complained of the excessive work.

Group data for either needs or press may be averaged and also presented in profile form. Figure 3 provides a contrast between the average press profile of seven liberal arts colleges, based on the responses of 460 upper-division students, and that obtained from 156 students from three business administration programs. The scores have been adjusted in these two profiles so that the value of five on any scale corresponds to the average score in a composite sample of 32 selected colleges and technical programs; any deviation from a perfect circle, therefore, indicates a deviation from the norm. It is reasonably clear from the two profiles that these liberal arts and business administration programs differ from other types of college programs as well as from one another. The business administration programs appear here as markedly higher in maintaining student *dependency needs,* particularly with respect to the press for *abasement, deference,* and *orderliness,* represented in the upper left sector of the circle (note the black ar-

(*Text continued on page 44.*)

Fig. 2—*Left*

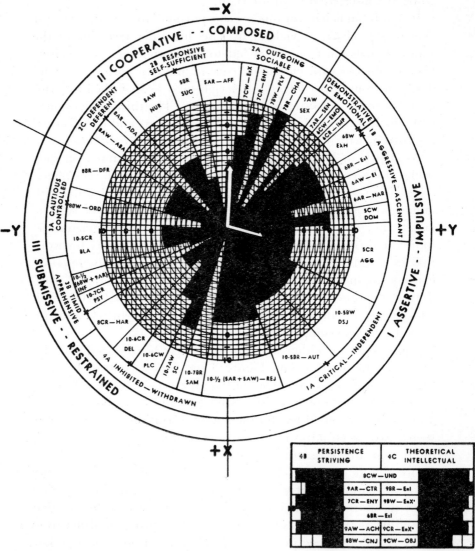

ACTIVITIES INDEX
FORM 156
DIAGNOSTIC SUMMARY

Fig. 2.—Needs scale profiles of two medical school freshmen. *Source:* George G. Stern and John S. Scanlon, "Pediatric Lions and Gynecological Lambs," *Journal of Medical Education,* XXXIII (1958), Part 2, 12–18.

FIG. 2—*Right*

ACTIVITIES INDEX
FORM 156
DIAGNOSTIC SUMMARY

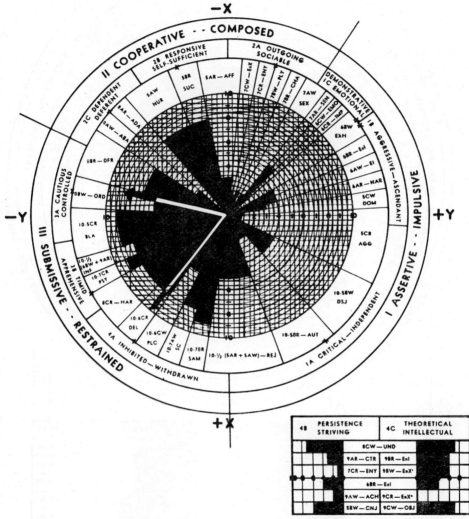

Copyright 1956 by George G. Stern

FIG. 3—*Left*

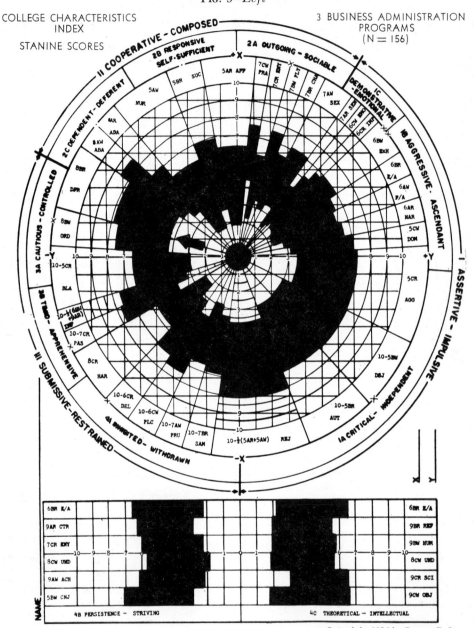

FIG. 3—Stanine score press scale profiles obtained from 460 students at seven liberal arts colleges and 156 students in three business administration programs. *Source:* George G. Stern, "Student Values and Their Relationship to the College Environment," in *Research on College Students,* ed. H. T. Sprague (Boulder, Colo.: Western Interstate Commission for Higher Education, 1960), pp. 67–104.

Fig. 3—*Right*

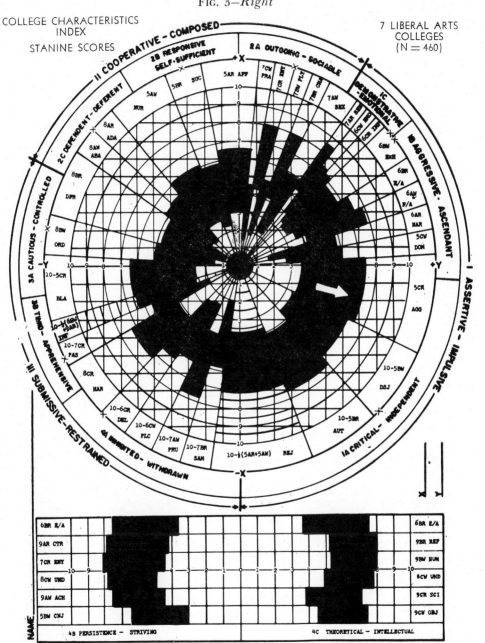

COLLEGE CHARACTERISTICS INDEX
STANINE SCORES

7 LIBERAL ARTS COLLEGES
(N = 460)

row.) The liberal arts colleges, on the other hand, are not only deficient in this area, but are in their turn correspondingly high in the *intellectual* areas summarized in the grid at the bottom of the figure.

Freshmen expectations.—Figure 4 shows the responses of the 317 selected freshmen who constituted the four subgroups described earlier, as contrasted with the 1,036 seniors. The senior profile is bounded by a solid line; the freshmen, by a dotted line cross-hatched in those areas where they exceed the seniors. Three general differences are apparent here:

1. The excess of senior scores in the lower right indicates that the freshmen expected to find less pressure toward establishing *personal independence* than the seniors describe as characteristic of the institution in question. The seniors, in fact, achieve a level of response well above the general college norm in this area, whereas the freshmen are equally far below it.

2. The excess of freshmen scores toward the upper right indicates that the freshmen expect to find much more pressure toward extreme forms of *emotional expression* than the seniors consider to be characteristic, although both are agreed in describing the school at a level which is above the norm in this respect.

3. There is a very considerable divergence between expectation and fact in regard to the *intellectual climate,* the freshmen anticipating an academic emphasis well above the general college norm, in contrast with the seniors, who describe the learning environment in terms that are generally below the norm.

Table 1 adds substance to the trends suggested by the freshmen profile; in it are reported the 99 items on the College Characteristics Index which at least 87.2 percent of the freshmen sample indicated they expected to find characteristic of the institution. There is an unmistakable emphasis here on the range and quality of instruction, the aspiration level of the students and the extensive opportunities for vigorous social participation.

The seniors, on the other hand, as shown in Table 2, not only agree on fewer unequivocal characteristics but also confine themselves almost entirely to items involving social participation. These are drawn predominantly from the *sex, play,* and *affiliation* scales,

(*Text continued on page 52.*)

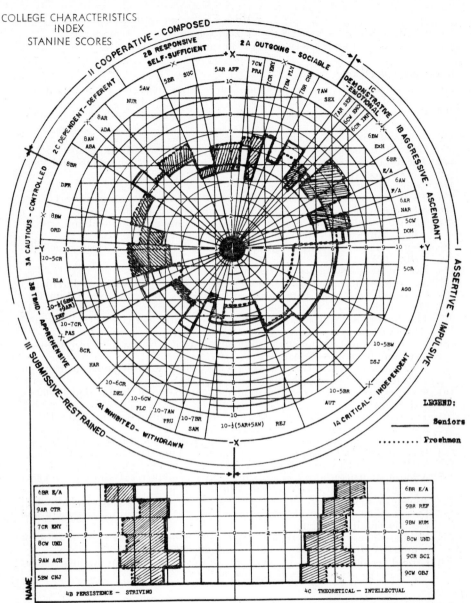

COLLEGE CHARACTERISTICS
INDEX
STANINE SCORES

Copyright 1956 by George G. Stern

FIG. 4—Profile contrasts between the expectations which 317 selected freshmen have of their college and a description of that school obtained from 1,036 graduating seniors.

45

TABLE 1

HIGH CONSENSUS ITEMS ON THE COLLEGE CHARACTERISTICS INDEX BY 317
SELECTED FRESHMEN FROM THE SAME COLLEGE†

I. *Intellectual climate*

270. Most of the professors are very thorough teachers and really probe into fundamentals of their subjects. (Und T)
193. Faculty members put a lot of energy and enthusiasm into their teaching. (Eny T*)
146. Course offerings and faculty in the natural sciences are outstanding. (Sci T)
236. Many of the natural science professors are actively engaged in research. (Sci T)
 26. The library is exceptionally well equipped with journals, periodicals, and books in the natural sciences. (Sci T*)
176. Laboratory facilities in the natural sciences are excellent. (Sci T*)
296. There is a lot of interest in the philosophy and methods of science. (Sci T)
 86. A lecture by an outstanding scientist would be poorly attended. (Sci F)
 47. The school offers many opportunities for students to understand and criticize important works in art, music, and drama. (Hum T)
 85. There are many facilities and opportunities for individual creative activity. (Ref T*)
115. Modern art and music get little attention here. (Ref F)
 77. A lecture by an outstanding literary critic would be poorly attended. (Hum F)
227. Course offerings and faculty in the social sciences are outstanding. (Hum T)
 17. Many of the social science professors are actively engaged in research. (Hum T)
257. The library is exceptionally well equipped with journals, periodicals, and books in the social sciences. (Hum T*)
131. There are practically no student organizations actively involved in campus or community affairs. (E/A F)
 71. Many students here develop a strong sense of responsibility about their role in contemporary social and political life. (E/A T)
161. Students are actively concerned about national and international affairs. (E/A T)
205. Tutorial or honors programs are available for qualified students. (Ref T)
272. Most courses are a real intellectual challenge. (Ach T)
 62. Most courses require intensive study and preparation out of class. (Ach T*)
 32. It is fairly easy to pass most courses without working very hard. (Ach F)
182. Students set high standards of achievement for themselves. (Ach T)
 67. A lot of students who get just passing grades at mid-term really make an effort to earn a higher grade by the end of the term. (Cnj T)
122. Students who work hard for high grades are likely to be regarded as odd. (Ach F)
152. Examinations here provide a genuine measure of a student's achievement and understanding. (Ach T)
240. In class discussions, papers, and exams, the main emphasis is on breadth of understanding, perspective, and critical judgment. (Und T)
300. Careful reasoning and clear logic are valued most highly in grading student papers, reports, or discussions. (Und T*)

---

† The code entry following each item indicates (*a*) the scale from which the item was obtained, (*b*) the direction of response (true or false), and (*c*) the level of consensus. All items listed in the table have been responded to in the same way by at least 87.2 percent of the subjects, corresponding to the .001 level of significance. Items which are further marked by an asterisk have been responded to in the same way by 95 percent of the subjects or more. Thus, the entry "(Und T)" signifies that the item comes from the Understanding scale, and that at least 87.2 percent (but not as many as 95 percent) of the subjects agreed that the item was true for this institution. A full list of scale names may be found in the stub of Tables 3 or 5.

TABLE 1—*continued*

II. *Dependency pressures*

290. This school has a reputation for being very friendly. (Nur T)
124. The school helps everyone get acquainted. (Aff T)
 20. Many upperclassmen play an active role in helping new students adjust to campus life. (Nur T)
157. Faculty advisers or counselors are pretty practical and efficient in the way they dispatch their business. (Cnj T)
 59. There is a student loan fund which is very helpful for minor emergencies. (Suc T)
299. Counseling and guidance services are really personal, patient, and extensive. (Suc T)
183. Students quickly learn what is done and not done on this campus. (Ada T*)
245. Students pay little attention to rules and regulations. (Agg F)
260. Chapel services on or near the campus are well attended. (Nur T)
 97. Activities in most student organizations are carefully and closely planned. (Cnj T)
119. Students here are encouraged to be independent and individualistic. (Suc T)
279. A controversial speaker always stirs up a lot of student discussion. (Dfr T)
  9. Students address faculty members as "professor" or "doctor." (Dfr T)
 52. Students must have a written excuse for absence from class. (Ord F)
 82. Student papers and reports must be neat. (Ord T*)
  7. Most courses are very well organized and progress systematically from week to week. (Cnj T*)
 37. Instructors clearly explain the goals and purposes of their courses. (Cnj T*)
232. Classrooms are kept clean and tidy. (Ord T)
262. Campus buildings are clearly marked by signs and directories. (Ord T)
  5. Students are conscientious about taking good care of school property. (Agg T)
172. The campus and buildings always look a little unkempt. (Ord F)
140. The college regards training people for service to the community as one of its major responsibilities. (Nur T)
230. Many church and social organizations are especially interested in charities and community services. (Nur T)

III. *Emotional expression*

204. The academic atmosphere is practical, emphasizing efficiency and usefulness. (Pra T)
135. Education here tends to make students more practical and realistic. (F/A T)
 54. There are psychology courses which deal in a practical way with personal adjustment and human relations. (Pra T*)
255. The future goals for most students emphasize job security, family happiness, and good citizenship. (F/A T*)
264. Education for leadership is strongly emphasized. (Pra T)
 74. Students have many opportunities to develop skill in organizing and directing the work of others. (Exh T)
 64. There are many opportunities for students to get together in extracurricular activities. (Aff T*)
  4. There are no fraternities or sororities. (Aff F*)
263. Students are very serious and purposeful about their work. (Ply T)
233. There isn't much to do here except go to classes and study. (Ply F*)
103. There are so many things to do here that students are busy all the time. (Eny T)
208. Students frequently go away for football games, skiing weekends, etc. (Sex T)
 83. There are lots of dances, parties, and social activities. (Ply T*)
 88. Most students here really enjoy dancing. (Sex T)

TABLE 1—*continued*

III. *Emotional expression*—continued

109. Most students here enjoy such activities as dancing, skating, diving, gymnastics. (Nar T)
102. There is a lot of excitement and restlessness just before holidays. (Emo T)
 53. The big college events draw a lot of student enthusiasm and support. (Ply T*)
 43. Students put a lot of energy into everything they do—in class and out. (Eny T)
282. Very few things here arouse much excitement or feeling. (Emo F)
 34. There is a lot of group spirit. (Aff T*)
284. Student parties are colorful and lively. (Exh T*)
 58. Student gathering places are typically active and noisy. (Sex T)
293. Every year there are carnivals, parades, and other festive events on campus. (Ply T*)
 11. Student pep rallies, parades, dances, carnivals, or demonstrations occur very rarely. (E/A F)
194. There is a lot of fanfare and pageantry in many of the college events. (Exh T)
289. Students think about dressing appropriately and interestingly for different occasions—classes, social events, sports, and other affairs. (Nar T*)
 48. New fads and phrases are continually springing up among the students. (Imp T)
258. There are frequent informal social gatherings. (Imp T)
214. Students spend a lot of time together at the snack bars, taverns, and in one another's rooms. (Aff T)
178. There are several popular spots where a crowd of boys and girls can always be found. (Sex T*)
203. It's easy to get a group together for card games, singing, going to the movies, etc. (Ply T)
 16. There is an extensive program of intramural sports and informal athletic activities. (Har T*)
216. The history and traditions of the college are strongly emphasized. (Cha F)
  6. The students here represent a great variety in nationality, religion, and social status. (Cha T*)
186. There are many foreign students on the campus. (Cha T)
 66. There are many students from widely different geographic regions. (Cha T)
126. Many students travel or look for jobs in different parts of the country during the summer. (Cha T)
164. It is easy to obtain student speakers for clubs or meetings. (Exh T)
 12. Students here learn that they are not only expected to develop ideals but also to express them in action. (Emo T*)
 40. Student elections generate a lot of intense campaigning and strong feeling. (Dom T)
 57. The college has invested very little in drama and dance. (Sen F)
229. Proper social forms and manners are important here. (Nar T)
 49. Students take a great deal of pride in their personal appearance. (Nar T)
 45. Students spend a lot of time planning their careers. (F/A T)
 15. Many famous people are brought to the campus for lectures, concerts, student discussions, etc. (F/A T)
285. Quite a few faculty members have had varied and unusual careers. (F/A T)
 10. There is a recognized group of student leaders on this campus. (Dom T)
130. The important people at this school expect others to show proper respect for them. (Dom T)

TABLE 2

I. Intellectual climate

131. There are practically no student organizations actively involved in campus or community affairs. (E/A F)
205. Tutorial or honors programs are available for qualified students. (Ref T)

II. Dependency pressures

183. Students quickly learn what is done and not done on this campus. (Ada T)
 82. Student papers and reports must be neat. (Ord T)

III. Emotional expression

234. The college offers many really practical courses such as typing, report writing, etc. (Pra T)
255. The future goals for most students emphasize job security, family happiness, and good citizenship. (F/A T)
 64. There are many opportunities for students to get together in extracurricular activities. (Aff T)
  4. There are no fraternities or sororities. (Aff F*)
233. There isn't much to do here except go to classes and study. (Ply F)
208. Students frequently go away for football games, skiing weekends, etc. (Sex T)
 83. There are lots of dances, parties, and social activities. (Ply T)
102. There is a lot of excitement and restlessness just before holidays. (Emo T*)
 58. Student gathering places are typically active and noisy. (Sex T)
293. Every year there are carnivals, parades, and other festive events on campus. (Ply T)
148. Bermuda shorts, pin-up pictures, etc. are common on this campus. (Sex T)
214. Students spend a lot of time together at the snack bars, taverns, and in one another's rooms. (Aff T)
 28. There is lots of informal dating during the week . . . at the library, snack bar, movies, etc. (Sex T)
178. There are several popular spots where a crowd of boys and girls can always be found. (Sex T)
203. It's easy to get a group together for card games, singing, going to the movies, etc. (Ply T)
 16. There is an extensive program of intramural sports and informal athletic activities. (Har T)
  6. The students here represent a great variety in nationality, religion, and social status. (Cha T)
186. There are many foreign students on the campus. (Cha T)
207. There are paintings or statues of nudes on campus. (Sen T)
259. Society orchestras are more popular here than jazz bands or novelty groups. (Nar F)
 15. Many famous people are brought to the campus for lectures, concerts, student discussions, etc. (F/A T)

* See footnote †, Table 1, for an explanation for the code entry following each item.

TABLE 3

Differences between the College Expectations of 317 Selected College Freshmen with Four Different High School Backgrounds and the College Descriptions Obtained from 1,086 Graduating Seniors, All at the Same College.*

Press Scales	High School Background								Total (N=317)		P_Ft†	College Senior Class (N=1,086)	
	63 Private (N=103)		42 Parochial (N=89)		1 Local Public (N=96)		1 Nonlocal Public (N=29)						
	X̄	σ	X̄	σ	X̄	σ	X̄	σ	X̄	σ		X̄	σ
Intellectual climate													
Achievement	6.86	1.03	6.99	1.06	+7.15	1.17	6.49	1.24	6.95	1.12	.05	3.34	1.99
Conjunctivity-Disjunctivity	6.42	1.14	6.49	.97	−5.84	1.59	6.25	1.58	6.25	1.32	.01	4.15	2.02
Counteraction-Infavoidance	5.63	1.98	5.81	1.76	5.40	1.95	5.49	1.25	5.60	1.85	—	3.98	1.94
Ego Achievement	7.53	1.56	7.55	1.53	7.77	1.48	7.87	1.33	7.64	1.51	—	6.00	2.00
Energy-Passivity	6.83	1.18	6.72	1.33	6.57	1.39	6.69	1.37	6.71	1.30	—	4.08	1.91
Humanism	6.75	1.30	6.81	1.23	6.69	1.37	6.86	1.20	6.76	1.29	—	5.01	1.73
Objectivity	5.56	1.53	5.25	1.64	5.77	1.46	5.59	1.56	5.54	1.55	—	3.94	2.08
Reflectiveness	6.97	1.42	6.99	1.25	7.16	1.28	6.84	1.52	7.02	1.36	—	5.28	1.80
Scientism	6.88	1.19	7.17	1.16	7.22	1.07	6.82	1.23	7.06	1.16	.05	4.41	1.92
Understanding	6.47	1.40	6.60	1.35	6.57	1.47	6.08	1.86	6.50	1.42	—	4.12	2.02
Dependency pressures													
Abasement	6.07	1.50	6.08	1.65	5.67	1.62	6.05	1.68	5.95	1.61	—	7.22	2.13
Adaptiveness	5.97	1.64	+6.84	1.49	5.85	1.74	5.49	1.55	6.14	1.66	.001	5.91	1.74
Affiliation-Rejection	6.39	1.48	6.43	1.70	6.16	1.60	6.34	1.54	6.33	1.58	—	4.61	1.94
Blameavoidance-Aggression	−5.89	1.85	6.10	1.61	6.63	1.41	6.09	1.51	6.19	1.65	.05	3.76	1.78
Conjunctivity-Disjunctivity	6.42	1.14	6.49	.97	5.84	1.59	6.25	1.58	6.25	1.32	.01	4.15	2.02
Deference	6.30	1.37	6.38	1.41	6.13	1.34	6.15	1.71	6.26	1.40	—	5.50	1.59
Nurturance-Rejection	6.80	1.55	6.80	1.50	7.06	1.19	6.89	1.21	6.89	1.40	—	5.55	1.83
Order	5.67	1.28	5.83	1.40	5.55	1.28	5.58	1.27	5.67	1.32	—	4.22	1.74
Succorance-Autonomy	4.95	1.67	5.39	1.80	5.04	1.52	5.54	1.17	5.15	1.65	—	4.63	1.81

* All values in this table are stanines (X̄ = 5.0, σ = 2.0) based on a normative sample of 1,993 upperclassmen in 32 American colleges. Deviations from 5.0 recorded above are correspondingly higher or lower than this criterion group.
† Means contributing to significant F are indicated by + and − signs (based on Duncan test).

TABLE 3—continued

Press Scales	63 Private (N=103)		42 Parochial (N=89)		1 Local Public (N=96)		1 Nonlocal Public (N=29)		Total (N=317)		P_F†	College Senior Class (N=1,036)	
	X̄	σ	X̄	σ	X̄	σ	X̄	σ	X̄	σ		X̄	σ
Emotional expression													
Aggression-Blameavoidance	+4.11	1.85	3.90	1.61	3.37	1.41	3.91	1.51	3.81	1.65	.05	6.24	1.78
Change-Sameness	5.69	1.44	5.53	1.12	5.80	1.29	5.52	1.36	5.66	1.32	—	5.51	1.52
Dominance	6.35	1.62	6.16	1.45	6.32	1.66	6.64	1.74	6.31	1.62	—	6.40	1.79
Ego Achievement	7.53	1.56	7.55	1.53	7.77	1.48	7.87	1.33	7.64	1.51	—	6.00	2.00
Emotionality-Placidity	6.35	1.49	6.38	1.45	6.41	1.62	6.44	1.19	6.39	1.48	—	4.59	1.88
Energy-Passivity	6.83	1.18	6.72	1.33	6.57	1.39	6.69	1.37	6.71	1.30	—	4.08	1.91
Exhibitionism-Infavoidance	7.96	1.28	6.97	1.32	7.95	1.37	7.83	1.44	7.95	1.32	—	5.42	2.06
Fantasied Achievement	6.20	1.71	6.44	1.68	6.80	1.46	5.95	1.89	6.43	1.66	.05	4.86	1.73
Impulsion-Deliberation	5.83	1.81	5.81	2.03	5.55	1.88	5.74	1.67	5.73	1.89	—	6.22	1.78
Narcissism	6.87	1.30	7.09	1.15	7.07	1.38	7.36	.92	7.04	1.25	—	5.56	1.71
Play	7.09	.79	6.86	.89	7.06	.73	+7.45	.75	7.05	.81	.01	7.00	1.38
Pragmatism	6.35	1.46	+7.04	1.32	6.62	1.31	6.41	1.05	6.63	1.37	.01	6.06	1.48
Risk-Harmavoidance	5.73	1.47	5.38	1.35	5.89	1.40	6.09	1.34	5.71	1.41	.05	6.43	1.34
Sentience	6.15	1.34	6.23	1.26	6.17	1.26	5.70	1.52	6.14	1.31	—	5.15	1.53
Sex-Prudishness	6.34	1.31	-6.10	1.53	6.75	1.22	6.98	1.24	6.46	1.36	.001	7.06	1.45

High School Background

51

unlike items selected by the freshmen, which suggest the expectation of a wider range of opportunity for emotional expressiveness.

As is shown in Table 3, there are relatively few differences between the four subgroups of freshmen in their expectations. The two largest discrepancies in this table are both associated with the parochial school graduates, who expect to be required to demonstrate a level of adaptive behavior which is as unrealistically high as their underestimate regarding sex activities is low, judged by the standards reported by the seniors.

High school–college continuity.—The responses given by these four groups of students to the High School Characteristics Index items, listed in Table 4, suggest an interesting relationship between the high schools from which these students came and the college which they have just entered. The high consensus of intellectual and dependency items suggests a relatively provocative and satisfying academic experience for these subjects at the secondary school level. It may be that the unrealistic expectations in these areas which they have for the college are based partly on assumptions derived from past experience. Evidently the freshmen agree on a number of favorable attributes of their high schools as learning environments. They are further agreed, as we have seen, that they expect to obtain much more of this same kind of satisfaction from their college experience, an expectation not borne out by the seniors.

It is of interest to note that there are a number of items describing sources of emotional and social expression that are common to all four types of high schools. These bear a strong similarity to the characteristics attributed to the college in question by both seniors and freshmen, although they are not nearly as extreme.

Variety among high schools.—In view of the foregoing, data summarized in Table 5 are of particular significance. Despite the fact that a very high percentage of entrants, regardless of high school background, have selected items suggesting an essentially satisfactory secondary school experience, Table 5 reveals some striking differences among the four types of high schools. The private schools, nondenominational and parochial, are described by

(*Text continued on page 56.*)

TABLE 4

HIGH CONSENSUS ITEMS ON THE HIGH SCHOOL CHARACTERISTICS INDEX BY 317
SELECTED FRESHMEN FROM THE SAME COLLEGE*

I. Intellectual climate

30. There is a lot of emphasis on preparing for college. (Und T)
205. Teachers welcome the student's own ideas on serious matters. (Ref T)
272. There are awards or special honors for those who do the best work or get the best grades. (Ach T)
68. Pupils are often expected to work at home on problems which they could not solve in class. (Ctr T)
300. Clear and careful thinking is most important in getting a good mark on reports, papers, and discussions. (Und T)
141. If a student thinks out a report carefully, teachers will give him a good mark even if they don't agree with him. (Obj T)

II. Dependency pressures

59. Outside of class most teachers are friendly and find time to chat with students. (Suc T)
1. Teachers are very interested in student ideas or opinions about school affairs. (Aba T)
275. Teachers seldom use physical punishment. (Agg T)
33. In gym class, all students must do the same exercises, no matter how good or bad they are at it. (Ada T)
247. It is hard to prepare for examinations because students seldom know what they will be tested on. (Cnj F)
127. Assignments are usually clear so everyone knows what to do. (Cnj T)
262. Offices and rooms are clearly marked. (Ord T*)
153. When a student fails a test, he has to take a note home to his parents. (Ada F)
215. There are frequent fights in the lunchroom or on the school grounds. (Agg F)

III. Emotional expression

204. Most students and their families think of education as a preparation for earning a good living. (Pra T)
84. This school offers very few really practical courses. (Pra F)
255. For most students, future goals emphasize job security, family happiness, and good citizenship. (F/A T)
4. There are very few clubs and student group activities to which students may belong. (Aff F)
88. Many students here really enjoy dancing. (Sex T)
102. Students can get into very heated arguments with one another, and be the best of friends the next day. (Emo T)
289. Students think about wearing the right clothes for different things—classes, social events, sports, and other affairs. (Nar T)
48. Students are always coming up with new fads and expressions. (Imp T)
143. New jokes and funny stories get around the school in a hurry. (Ply T)
148. Boys and girls often get together between classes, during lunch hour, etc. (Sex T)
65. Most students can easily keep out of trouble in this school. (Agg T)
133. Teachers here have little interest in what they are doing. (Eny F)
76. Fire drills and civil defense drills are held regularly. (Har T*)
259. Teachers are always carefully dressed and neatly groomed. (Nar T)
49. Students take a great deal of pride in their personal appearance. (Nar T)
15. In English classes, students are encouraged to be imaginative when they write. (F/A T)
10. There is a recognized group of student leaders at this school. (Dom T)
8. Teachers often try to get students to speak up freely and openly in class. (Ctr T)

* See footnote †, Table 1, for an explanation of the code entry following each item.

TABLE 5
Differences in High School Descriptions by 317 College Freshmen from Four Types of Secondary Schools*

Press Scales	High School Background											P_F†
	63 Private (N=103)		42 Parochial (N=89)		1 Local Public (N=96)		1 Nonlocal Public (N=29)		Total (N=317)		
	$\overline{X}$	σ	$\overline{X}$	σ	$\overline{X}$	σ	$\overline{X}$	σ	$\overline{X}$	σ	
Intellectual climate											
Achievement	+6.15	1.87	5.75	2.21	5.14	1.86	4.94	1.97	5.62	1.72	.01
Conjunctivity-Disjunctivity	6.04	1.44	5.70	1.53	−4.64	2.04	−4.73	1.66	5.40	1.80	.001
Counteraction-Infavoidance	5.96	1.62	+5.11	2.11	4.07	2.42	3.68	1.93	4.94	2.23	.001
Ego Achievement	5.97	1.79	5.19	2.26	5.51	1.85	4.60	1.92	5.49	2.00	.01
Energy-Passivity	6.15	1.85	5.62	2.07	5.25	2.02	4.04	2.05	5.24	2.14	.001
Humanism	+6.46	2.10	5.15	2.16	4.83	1.76	5.16	1.49	5.48	2.09	.001
Objectivity	+5.58	1.74	5.06	1.88	4.50	2.26	4.81	2.08	5.04	2.02	.001
Reflectiveness	+6.35	1.56	5.60	1.90	5.90	1.82	5.00	1.97	5.64	1.85	.01
Scientism	5.26	1.79	4.69	2.22	5.26	1.64	5.54	1.45	5.13	1.86	.001
Understanding	+6.21	1.72	+5.41	1.98	−4.60	2.06	−4.52	1.52	5.35	1.99	.001
Dependency pressures											
Abasement	4.63	1.88	5.18	2.01	+5.68	2.17	5.32	2.26	5.17	2.08	.01
Adaptiveness	4.84	1.85	5.14	1.92	4.64	2.21	4.18	1.50	4.80	1.99	
Affiliation-Rejection	4.44	2.24	4.70	2.43	4.68	2.12	−1.85	2.32	4.35	2.40	.001
Blameavoidance-Aggression	5.68	1.74	5.61	1.61	5.62	1.70	−4.49	1.66	5.53	1.71	.05
Conjunctivity-Disjunctivity	6.04	1.44	5.70	1.53	4.64	2.04	4.73	1.66	5.40	1.80	.001
Deference	4.93	2.28	+6.83	2.18	4.78	2.26	4.89	1.69	5.41	2.38	.001
Nurturance-Rejection	+5.81	1.69	+6.47	1.35	−5.04	1.88	−4.00	1.45	5.60	1.80	.001
Order	−4.99	2.00	+6.75	1.75	5.77	1.76	5.50	1.63	5.77	1.95	.001
Succorance-Autonomy	+5.37	1.75	+5.52	1.73	−2.96	2.14	−2.80	2.41	4.45	2.29	.001

* All values in this table are stanines ($\overline{X}=5.0$, σ=2.0) based on a normative random sample of 210 freshmen at the same college. Deviations from 5.0 recorded above are correspondingly higher or lower than this criterion group.
† Means contributing to significant F are indicated by + and − signs (based on Duncan's test).

TABLE 5—*continued*

| PRESS SCALES | HIGH SCHOOL BACKGROUND | | | | | | | | | | | | P_F† |
| | 63 Private (N=103) | | 42 Parochial (N=89) | | 1 Local Public (N=96) | | 1 Nonlocal Public (N=29) | | TOTAL (N=317) | | |
	X̄	σ	X̄	σ	X̄	σ	X̄	σ	X̄	σ	
Emotional expression											
Aggression-Blameavoidance	4.32	1.74	4.39	1.61	4.38	1.70	+5.51	1.66	4.47	1.71	.05
Change-Sameness	5.80	1.92	5.14	1.77	−4.40	1.70	−3.73	1.86	5.00	1.93	.001
Dominance	−4.35	1.98	−4.44	2.02	−5.63	1.87	5.82	1.58	4.90	2.02	.001
Ego Achievement	+5.97	1.79	5.19	2.26	5.51	1.85	4.60	1.92	5.49	2.00	.01
Emotionality-Placidity	+5.61	1.95	+5.65	1.81	4.34	2.08	3.07	1.98	5.00	2.14	.001
Energy-Passivity	+6.15	1.85	+5.62	2.07	4.25	2.02	4.04	2.05	5.24	2.14	.001
Exhibitionism-Infavoidance	4.77	1.89	4.91	2.03	5.34	1.86	4.59	1.60	4.97	1.91	.001
Fantasied Achievement	5.19	1.18	4.77	1.03	5.08	1.03	4.79	1.15	5.00	1.12	
Impulsion-Deliberation	4.21	2.49	4.10	2.01	4.48	2.03	+5.54	1.76	4.39	2.19	.05
Narcissism	4.95	2.19	+5.58	1.49	4.66	1.64	4.69	1.22	5.02	1.80	.01
Play	4.08	2.05	4.84	2.06	4.75	1.56	−2.86	2.37	4.39	2.03	.001
Pragmatism	3.57	2.36	4.27	2.28	+5.25	1.81	3.83	1.87	4.30	2.25	.001
Risk-Harmavoidance	4.19	1.92	−3.56	1.61	+5.65	1.69	4.73	1.76	4.50	1.93	.001
Sentience	+5.80	1.67	4.76	2.04	4.50	1.72	4.52	1.18	5.00	1.84	.001
Sex-Prudery	−3.24	2.49	3.55	1.70	5.32	1.55	+5.35	1.36	4.15	2.16	.001

55

their graduates as offering considerably greater intellectual stimulation than is the case for either of the public school samples. This difference is all the more noteworthy since both public schools are known for their high-quality programs and the large percentage of their graduates who go on to college. The private preparatory schools stand out strongly on every academically oriented scale with the exception of science, a peculiar absence that has also been noted by McArthur[19] in his analysis of private school students at Harvard.

The parochial schools are noteworthy for the emphasis placed on dependency and conformity. This has also been found to characterize denominational colleges, regardless of religious affiliation (Stern[20]). Both public schools suggest fairly consistent trends toward personal autonomy.

Differences between the most extreme types of schools in the present sample, the private preparatory versus the nonlocal metropolitan public, are shown in profile form in Figure 5. The private school profile is bounded by a solid line; the public school, by a dotted line crosshatched in those areas where it exceeds the private school. Both trends referred to previously are brought out clearly in the profile. The excess scores of the public school graduates in the lower right portion of the circle indicate a greater degree of independence and an absence of dependency relationships between teacher and pupil in the public high school. The intellectual scores recorded in the grid at the bottom are consistently in favor of the private preparatory school. Both factors seem likely to be a function of the considerably greater size and bureaucratization of the public school involved.

CONCLUSIONS

The present paper has described a technique for quantifying certain psychological aspects of school environments, both secondary and college. The results reported here are limited by the

---

[19] C. McArthur, "Subculture and Personality during the College Years," *Journal of Educational Sociology*, XXXIII (1960), 260–68.

[20] Stern, "Student Values and Their Relationship to the College Environment," in *Research on College Students;* also "Environments for Learning," in *The American College.*

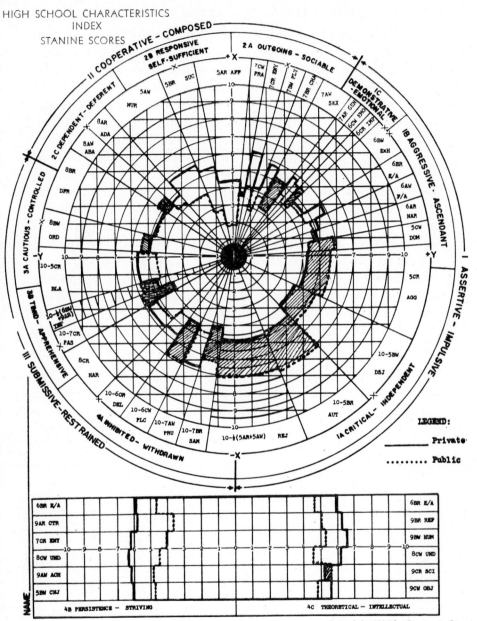

HIGH SCHOOL CHARACTERISTICS
INDEX
STANINE SCORES

FIG. 5.—Profile contrasts between high school descriptions of 103 private preparatory school graduates and 29 metropolitan public high school graduates of comparable socioeconomic class level.

preliminary nature of one of the two tests utilized (the High School Characteristics Index was administered for the first time here) as well as by the restrictiveness of the sample. As the instrument is improved and the range of high school samples broadened to include students who have not gone on to college, the differences between high schools should become even more sharply delineated.

In the light of these limitations the present findings are all the more striking. Graduates from four strong high school programs describe a satisfying secondary school experience but indicate their high hopes for a far more challenging experience in college. This expectation is not associated with a wholly unrealistic appraisal of the school in question—they are quite accurately aware of the spirited social atmosphere at this institution. The students come expecting to learn; they learn not to expect so much. These data suggest that student apathy is the *consequence* of unfulfilled expectations in the transition from high school to college, rather than the cause. We need to raise our sights somewhat higher, at least to the level that the entering freshman apparently sets for himself.

RECENT RESEARCH ON INSTITUTIONAL CLIMATES: 2

The Vocational College Culture

T. R. McCONNELL
*Chairman, Center for the Study of Higher Education,
University of California, Berkeley*

R ECENT RESEARCH, both on student characteristics and on college environments, has exposed the limited usefulness—one might almost say the meaninglessness—of our conventional typologies of higher institutions. Even large universities may not be as distinct from small liberal arts colleges as one would suppose. The two groups of institutions obviously are different in complexity as well as in size. But in the attitudes of faculty and students toward the basic purposes and values of higher education they may be quite similar. Both small liberal arts colleges and large, complex institutions may be oriented more toward vocational training or vocational careers than toward commerce in ideas.

From a study of curricular changes since 1870, in fifty small or medium-sized independent liberal arts colleges, McGrath and Russell concluded that vocational or professional programs "which differ in the degree of specialization in no substantial respect from comparable programs offered in undergraduate *professional* schools are now almost invariably a part of the offerings of the liberal arts colleges studied." They suggested, also, that vocationalism had invaded the traditional liberal disciplines. As evidence they cited the fact that in many departments of small liberal arts colleges the total number of credit hours offered exceeds the number required for a major by four or five times.[1]

[1] E. J. McGrath and C. H. Russell, *Are Liberal Arts Colleges Becoming Profes-*

Undue specialization is not the only evidence of the professionalization of the liberal arts college. "In a measure the graduate schools deny society the services which the colleges ought to perform," charged McGrath, "by transforming them from institutions for general education into agencies for the initial vocational education of scholars. They produce college teachers prepared not primarily for their chosen work but rather for research activities of a limited character."[2]

In spirit and orientation, then, both liberal arts colleges and universities may have much in common. In this sense the classification system is basically faulty.

The usual typology is also unsatisfactory within categories. Enormous differences in character exist among private universities that are comparable in structure. Thus Syracuse is not Harvard; neither is it Stanford, Chicago, or even Buffalo. Great variation may be found among state universities. Michigan State University is not the University of Michigan. The atmosphere at Minnesota differs greatly from that at California. It is true that the state universities resemble one another in many ways, but their differences often impress one much more than their similarities.

DIVERSITY AMONG LIBERAL ARTS COLLEGES

Diversity also characterizes institutions that are lumped together as liberal arts colleges. The Center for the Study of Higher Education at Berkeley has estimated the selectivity of American higher education as a whole, the relative selectivity of certain types or groups of institutions, and the variation in average scholastic aptitude among the institutions in each of the categories. In one of the states the center has studied intensively, only about 16 percent of the freshmen in the least selective institution had scores above the average score in the most selective one. Both are separate liberal arts colleges. Although the two colleges profess comparable objectives and are similar structurally, it is obvious that they are dissimilar indeed in the intellectual demands they can make on their students. The most selective college sends many students on

---

sional Schools? (New York: Bureau of Publications, Teachers College, Columbia University, 1958).

[2] E. J. McGrath, The Graduate School and the Decline of Liberal Education (New York: Bureau of Publications, Teachers College, Columbia University, 1959).

to professional and graduate schools. The other sends few. Although the curricular pattern of the two institutions is much the same, their students and faculties live in very different worlds.

Consider the variation in the ability of entering students among the Protestant and independent liberal arts colleges in the North Central region. Among the North Central colleges which fell into the center's national sample of institutions, the average freshman scholastic aptitude test scores ranged from 90 to 121.[3] In the South, the range for the same combination of colleges was from 74 to 123. In the latter group, the range of average scores was almost as great as the range within which two-thirds of the individual freshman scores in the country fell.[4] Heterogeneous as they are in student ability, liberal arts colleges do not comprise a very meaningful institutional type.

STUDENT DETERMINANTS OF ORGANIZATIONAL CHARACTER

Scholastic ability and other student characteristics play an influential role in determining the atmosphere or climate of a college. As Clark has observed, these characteristics "set many of the terms under which organizational work is done."[5] In his case study of an unselective California public junior college, Clark found that the range of ability among the students was great and the average low; for example, only 7 percent of the students were above the 80th percentile on the national norms of a scholastic aptitude test, and 42 percent scored below the 20th percentile. The students came predominantly from working-class families; less than a fourth of the local students were from business and professional families, whereas two-thirds came from "blue-collar" backgrounds. Two-thirds of the students enrolled in transfer programs, but only a third of them, about 22 percent of those who entered the college, actually transferred to four-year institutions. Clark called the professed transfer students who did not go on to senior

---

[3] The general mean of all freshmen in the national sample was 104; the standard deviation, 27.

[4] T. R. McConnell, "Differential Selectivity of American Higher Education," in *The Coming Crisis in the Selection of Students for College Entrance,* ed. K. E. Anderson (Washington: American Educational Research Association, 1960).

[5] B. R. Clark, *The Open Door College: A Case Study* (New York: McGraw-Hill Book Co., 1960), p. 11. (One of a series of studies on diversity in American higher education made at the Center for the Study of Higher Education, Berkeley.)

institutions the "latent terminals." While the college had to do its best to prepare the real transfer student to perform acceptably in a four-year college—its reputation in the community depended in large part on its success in this function—much of its energy was expended in processing the latent terminals. Clark characterized this as a "cooling-out" procedure, in which by various devices the junior college staff attempted to persuade the student to relinquish his original intention and to move from the transfer program into a vocational or semiprofessional curriculum lasting for two years or less. This process, said Clark, makes of the junior college "a classification and distribution center from which large numbers of students leave education after a relatively short stay."[6]

The mass clientele of the college, the high degree of attrition in the student body, the necessity for reorienting a large proportion of the students, the open-door policy in admission, and the college's ambiguous role in the educational system conjoined to make it difficult for the college to attain a clear identity; to create in the minds of students, faculty, parents, and community a distinct image; to define its role clearly and realistically; and to attain organizational autonomy. Clark has summarized the consequences of this blurring of status and role as follows:

Along a continuum of organizational power in environmental relations, ranging from the organization that dominates its environmental relations to one completely dominated by its environment, the public junior college tends strongly toward the latter extreme.

Like state universities and state colleges, junior colleges can somewhat diminish their vulnerability by internal devices. All students must be admitted, but then they can be differentially treated; for example, criteria for admission to various programs can be established, to control better the impact of students on the program structure. But the foremost issue in the control of a constituency is who is to have access to membership. The mass college will elaborate internal processing devices precisely to attain some self-direction, but the basic source of the problem of autonomy remains. The power to select a social base is to be seen as the ultimate variable in the determination of the character of the public two-year college.[7]

On other occasions, in discussing the salient traits of college students, I have suggested ways in which characteristics other than

[6] *Ibid.,* p. 85.
[7] *Ibid.,* pp. 176–77.

general scholastic aptitude tend to mold the college environment. Our data have been derived mainly from studies of the differential selectivity of higher institutions in students' social and cultural backgrounds, interests, and motivations, and intellectual dispositions.

In Minnesota, the state colleges and the junior colleges are attended predominantly by students whose fathers are in low-status occupations. Dr. J. G. Darley's investigation for the center showed, for example, that only 27 percent of the men and 21 percent of the women in the state colleges had fathers in managerial or higher positions on the occupational scale. In the private and Protestant liberal arts colleges, on the other hand, 54 and 56 percent of the men and women, respectively, had fathers in the high-status category. The difference in attitudes, beliefs, values, interest in and familiarity with ideas associated with differences in status must create profound differences in the dominant climates and educational tasks of institutions with high and low concentrations of students from upper or lower classes.[8]

Let me turn now to differential selectivity and attraction in certain intellectual bents and dispositions—characteristics which, in our samples, have only a modest correlation with general scholastic aptitude. Dr. John Holland reported some time ago that the students who win awards from the National Merit Scholarship Corporation tend to enter institutions that have been highly productive in the sense that a large proportion of their graduates have earned the doctorate, and that the fifty most productive institutions get far more than their proportionate share of the ablest NMS students.[9]

In a report to appear soon in *Science,* the Center for the Study of Higher Education will show that the highly productive institutions also tend to attract NMS students with higher scores on certain measures of personality and intellectual disposition. In this case, two groups of NMS students with equal average scholastic aptitude test scores were studied, one of which had entered highly productive and the other, less productive colleges. Those

---

[8] Unpublished manuscript; Center for the Study of Higher Education, University of California, Berkeley.

[9] Holland, "Undergraduate Origins of American Scientists," *Science,* CXXVI (1957), 433–37.

who attended the more productive institutions could be described as more flexible, more tolerant of ambiguity, more complex in their perception of the environment, more intrinsically interested in ideas, more theoretically inclined, and potentially more creative.

The center has found that on a test of thinking introversion designed to measure intrinsic interest in ideas—that is, interest in ideas as such rather than in their practical applications—NMS students who attended public universities had lower scores than those who went to certain groups of liberal arts colleges, Ivy League universities, and other private institutions. The center matched on scholastic aptitude and intended field of specialization forty NMS men who attended Catholic institutions with forty each who entered public, Protestant, and private institutions. Those who entered the Catholic colleges were significantly higher on authoritarianism and significantly lower on tests of originality, complexity of outlook, and thinking introversion than those who went to the other groups of institutions.[10]

Without doubt, large concentrations of students with theoretical, complex, creative, and flexible intellectual bents will give a decided cast to a college. Large numbers of students who are practically oriented; rigid, conventional, and literal in outlook; or authoritarian in disposition, will create quite a different atmosphere. The characteristics of students are not the only determinants of institutional climate, but they must be among the more potent factors in giving a college a distinctive character.

It is generally known that the California Institute of Technology is extremely selective and that its student body is highly homogeneous in scholastic aptitude. The institute also draws a high proportion of students with theoretical interests, although it also attracts students with a definite applied orientation. Members of the staff of the Center for the Study of Higher Education have recently completed a study of the personality differences between Cal Tech high and low achievers who were equated on scholastic aptitude. Three times as many high as low achievers

[10] McConnell, *op. cit.* See also T. R. McConnell and Paul Heist, "Do Students Make the College?" *College and University*, XXXV (1959), 442–52.

had a theoretical, creative orientation. Conversely, twice as many low as high achievers had an applied, professional bias.[11]

There is some circumstantial evidence that Cal Tech is more interested in scientists than in engineers. Some members of the faculty have been heard to say that the institute draws too many students with applied rather than theoretical dispositions. The fact that students with a theoretical turn of mind get higher grades than those with applied bents suggests that the faculty rewards students who approach their problems theoretically rather than practically, or that the faculty sets the kinds of tasks that students with applied dispositions find less congenial than students who are more theoretically inclined.

There are other straws in the same wind. On the Stern-Pace College Characteristics Index, devised to get at students' perception of the press of college environments, National Merit Scholarship students at Cal Tech detected less emphasis on pragmatic values in their institution than did students at four fairly typical engineering schools. Furthermore, the scores on the scales for understanding and objectivity were higher at Cal Tech than at the four other institutions. Perhaps not all students who choose Cal Tech have a clear image of its dominant characteristics before they enter.

Vocationalism in Higher Education

Evidence of differential selectivity in educational values will take us back to the subject of vocationalism in higher education.

In the Cornell University study of values, students in several colleges and universities were asked to choose from a list of possible educational goals those they thought the ideal institution should emphasize. Students at Wesleyan, Yale, Harvard, and Dartmouth were most likely to check "basic general education and appreciation of ideas" and least likely to mark "vocational training." On the other hand, men at the state universities checked vocational preparation much more frequently than those at the

[11] P. A. Heist and P. A. Williams, "Variation in Achievement within a Select and Homogenous Student Body" (Unpublished paper; Center for the Study of Higher Education, University of California, Berkeley).

Ivy League colleges.[12] For example, at the extremes, 90 percent of the Wesleyan and 88 percent of the Yale students, and 65 and 64 percent of the University of Texas and Wayne men, respectively, said that "general education and appreciation of ideas" was a highly important emphasis. On the other hand, whereas only 36 and 31 percent of the Wesleyan and Yale students agreed that vocational training was highly important, 67 and 74 percent of the Texas and Wayne men gave it pre-eminence.

The Center for the Study of Higher Education has asked the same question of students at eight institutions; data from four of them are at hand. The percentages of freshmen (men and women together) who checked vocational training as of first importance were as follows: Swarthmore, 25; Antioch, 25; Reed, 14; and San Francisco State, 67. The percentages who considered general education and appreciation of ideas most important were Swarthmore, 54; Antioch, 50; Reed, 70; and San Francisco State, 23.

We do not yet have any data on changes in point of view during college at these four institutions, but we do have some cross-sectional data. The percentages of freshmen and seniors who considered vocational training as of paramount importance were as follows: Swarthmore, 25 and 8; Antioch, 25 and 13; Reed, 14 and 14; San Francisco State, 67 and 50. The percentages of the two classes that gave first place to general education and appreciation of ideas were: Swarthmore, 54 and 85; Antioch, 50 and 75; Reed, 70 and 76; and San Francisco State, 23 and 42. Except for Reed, there was a substantial difference between freshmen and seniors in value placed on general education and interest in ideas.

The center has some comparable data for approximately nine hundred men and women who received National Merit Scholarship Corporation awards in 1956. About half of those who entered public institutions said they thought the ideal college should be primarily concerned with vocational training, whereas only 25 percent of those who went to private and Protestant institutions and 17 percent of those who attended Roman Catholic institutions were of the same mind. Contrariwise, only 38 percent of the NMS students who chose public institutions thought that the ideal

[12] R. K. Goldsen et al., What College Students Think (Princeton, N.J.: D. Van Nostrand Co., 1960), p. 208.

college should stress intellectual values; but 60, 53, and 40 percent, respectively, of those who entered the other three groups of institutions considered intellectual objectives to be paramount.

The center has longitudinal data for 504 NMS students, although the responses have not been divided by institutional groups. In the summer of 1956, before these students entered college, 33 percent checked vocational training as the most important objective of an ideal college; after being in college two years, only 17 percent, or about half as many, expressed the same opinion. The percentages who checked general education and appreciation of ideas as most important increased from 50 to 71. The trend is thus in the same direction as that suggested by the cross-sectional analysis. Either college experience changes the relative value students place on these two objectives, or they learn what the faculty wants them to say.

Dr. Burton R. Clark and Dr. Martin Trow, sociologists at the Center for the Study of Higher Education, have identified four kinds of student cultures or subcultures: the academic, the vocational, the nonconformist, and the collegiate.[13]

This typology is not greatly different from that at which Dr. C. Robert Pace arrived through an analysis of students' responses on the thirty scales of the College Characteristics Index in thirty-two colleges. Pace distinguished the following types of environments: the intellectual; the practical and status oriented; the human relations, group welfare oriented; and the rebellious.[14] The Clark-Trow academic culture corresponds roughly to the intellectual, except that Pace found that there are two kinds of intellectual press, one particularly favorable to attainment in humanistic studies, and the other to achievement in the sciences. The vocational and the practical, status-oriented environments may be roughly equated, and the nonconformist and rebellious cultures presumably are much alike. The collegiate culture of Clark and Trow, however, is not comparable to the group-welfare type identified by Pace. In an instrument designed to reveal subcultures

[13] Clark and Trow, "Determinants of College Student Subcultures" (a chapter prepared for the forthcoming volume on the study of peer group influences, ed. Theodore Newcomb).

[14] Pace, "Five College Environments," *College Board Review*, Spring 1960, pp. 24–28.

rather than dominant general environments, Pace has tentatively included a scale dealing with playfulness, which presumably overlaps considerably with the "collegiate" culture.[15] In what follows I shall be concerned mainly with vocational cultures and subcultures.

Clark and Trow point out that the vocational culture is especially dominant in urban institutions attended for the most part by young people from working and lower-middle-class homes who are ambitious for higher social and economic status. "To these students, many of them married, most of them working anywhere from 20 to 40 hours a week," these authors say, "college is largely off-the-job training, an organization of courses and credits leading to a diploma and a better job than they could otherwise command." For such students, "college is an adjunct to the world of jobs," and they are "resistant to intellectual demands on them beyond what is required to pass the courses."[16]

It may be said in passing that this attitude toward the academic program is not confined to undergraduates. It has been found in a study of student culture in a medical school. Confronted with far more material than they believed they could learn, the medical students devised methods of reducing the curriculum to manageable proportions. At first they took one of two points of view: one group decided that they should concentrate on what they would need to know in medical practice—in this case general practice; the other group took the tack of trying to find out what they needed to know to pass the examinations. After the first tests, they reappraised their positions and decided that the best strategy was to learn "basic medical facts," which were important in practice and which, if the faculty was "reasonable," would appear on examinations. In winnowing the wheat from the chaff, they shunned theoretical concepts and the findings of research that were not yet in clinical use on the ground that these were not facts and were not useful to medical students.

These attitudes were carried into the clinical years, during which they considered anything unrelated to familiarity with the

[15] Pace, "The College Characteristics Analysis: Preliminary Comments" (Mimeographed; Syracuse: Higher Education Research Center, Syracuse University).
[16] Clark and Trow, *op. cit.*

diseases they might expect to encounter in general practice to be irrelevant. During this period students often decided for themselves what was a reasonable amount of work—an appropriate number of clinical case histories to prepare, for example—and had enough group solidarity to substitute this amount for the greater number of histories the faculty had assigned. The sociologists who conducted the study concluded that the medical student culture "provides them with sufficient collective support to allow them to direct their effort in quite different directions than those suggested by the faculty."[17]

That both urban universities and large, complex state colleges and universities that offer many kinds of occupational training attract large cohorts of vocationally minded students, is well supported by the data summarized above on what students in different kinds of institutions considered to be the most important goals of college education. Clark and Trow observed that proponents of the vocational and practical—and I should add, even the anti-intellectual—values of college may be found in the faculties as well as in the student bodies of these institutions.

In testimony thereof, I submit the following paragraphs from a letter concurred in by nine members of one of the departments of a large, multipurpose state college:

Now a middle-class student who attends a college or university in the United States is strongly motivated to "amount to something," and he sees a university education as an avenue of social mobility through which he can better his status socially as well as economically. He demands an education that he understands, that has some purpose or end that he can accept, and attach value to. Knowledge for the middle-class student has to be of some use.

There was a concession in the letter to the need for general education:

I am compelled to believe that the undergraduate student in our society needs certain essential knowledge from the various disciplines of the liberal arts. He also needs to develop certain abilities, to gain information, to adopt certain attitudes that will help him to gain his own goals. It is the function of higher education . . . to provide the instruction that will make this possible.

[17] H. S. Becker and B. Geer, "Student Culture in Medical School," *Harvard Educational Review*, XXVIII (1958), 70–80.

But in the next breath, the writer asserted that the customer has a right to buy what he wants:

It is my contention that the state college system has the same ends as the public school system. Partly my argument has to do with the purpose of education in America, and with this the idea that the consumer of goods should be able to get what he thinks he is paying for. . . .

Public education in the United States is viewed, here, as a public service somewhat similar to the other public services that the public taxes itself to provide. That is, the society is buying a service, and it is the right of a society to determine what kind, and how much, of this service they wish to provide. . . . The society that pays the bills is going to get, in the end, the kind of education it pays for.

One of the signers had this to say in another letter:

We do not see . . . college as an island of irresponsible but articulate critics in a desert of barbarism. We believe that we must take students able to meet our admission standards and enhance their professional and occupational goals with as much of science, the humanities, and the social sciences as they economically can afford and intellectually can accommodate. . . .

The implication is that the vocational purposes and programs of the college should be central and the liberal arts peripheral. This is without question the hierarchy of values which many a public institution exemplifies.

The implication in the last paragraph I quoted is also that the college should not tamper with the values and attitudes students bring with them. In these regards, the students should leave as they came.

While lower-middle-class origins dispose students to embrace vocationalism, upper-middle-class backgrounds, according to Clark and Trow, create "aspirations for the intellectual occupations and professions that involve postgraduate study" and direct students toward "the academic culture and the discipline of learning." They point out that these undergraduates' professional motivation is less narrow, direct, and immediate. These students have time and money—and in many instances, I am sure, the inclination —to spend four years on "general education and appreciation of ideas." But that they are basically less vocationally motivated than students from humbler homes is debatable. Riesman has observed that many of the students in elite colleges which send a large number of students on for advanced study "are already little dons, ready to start graduate school at the beginning of their freshman year. They are already so 'academic' in the good and bad connotations of the word that they may not change much in college, save to become still more erudite."[18]

And as McGrath has pointed out, the liberal arts college will with alacrity give the future dons their initial vocational education.

Clark and Trow assert that relatively high selectivity in academic ability is a necessary, although not a sufficient, condition for the development of a pervasive academic culture: "Selectivity brings a clientele that at least has the potential ability for difficult study and vigorous intellectual life; the selective college may also select for seriousness."[19] Beyond selectivity, institutional and intellectual autonomy are required. By this they mean that the college espouses values that may not be prized by society generally and that at the price of being different from many other institutions the college holds tenaciously to the conviction that liberal education has a central rather than a marginal importance in our society.

Clark and Trow also state that a college is likely to develop a dominant academic culture when the campus constitutes a community. This suggests that the intellectual life is most likely to prevail in a selective, distinctive, relatively small, residential college (although they believe that some adaptations can be made in large institutions to simulate a smaller elite community for academically motivated undergraduates).

It should be remembered that Clark and Trow were writing about academically elite liberal arts colleges. I should like to emphasize, as I did in the beginning, that there is no assurance that a self-styled liberal arts college is worthy of the name, for many become vocationalized by offering specific occupational training. Let me give you a few examples.

In an Ohio private college with an enrollment of 1,200, more

[18] D. Riesman, "College Subcultures and College Outcomes," in *Selection and Educational Differentiation,* ed. T. R. McConnell (Berkeley: Field Service Center and Center for the Study of Higher Education, University of California, 1960); pp. 1–14.
[19] Clark and Trow, *op. cit.*

than 400 students were preparing to teach; those who were going
into elementary education were required to take 70 quarter credits
in professional courses. More than 250 students were specializing
in the division of commerce. A random sample showed graduates
in commerce had taken from 58 to 100 credits in that division,
with 75 credits as the median. A highly professionalized conserva-
tory of music had attracted 160 majors. Of the 186 quarter hours
required for the bachelor of music or the bachelor of music education degree, only 45 were allocated to general education while
141 were reserved for professional work.

In a Southern liberal arts college, the largest numbers of majors
among the seniors of 1958 were in geology (which emphasized
petroleum geology) , commerce, physical education, and education.
This college, which had 760 students at the time, offered 40 semester hours in accounting. The college actually solicited students
who had a strong vocational motivation. The dean prepared a
memorandum for the public relations staff which stated that more
than 60 percent of the course work taken at the college was of an
"up-to-date, practical nature" ranging from use of the slide rule
to oil and gas law, first aid, electronics, and sedimentation. Such
courses were said to prepare men for immediate practical employ-
ment. A list of pertinent courses and student enrollments was
given, in which the largest registrations were in accounting and
auditing (189 students), and business operations, including business law, business correspondence, salesmanship, credit and col-
lections, and corporation finance (135 students) .

The dean's memorandum declared that "liberal arts is what
you make it. It can be pre-Shakespearean drama or well-logging.
Or it can be both. At this college it is both."

In fairness it should be said that the memorandum stated that
the college required a balanced program, with a rather large block
of required work distributed over the principal fields of knowledge. It also asserted that the college avoided "how-to" instruction
and emphasized the ability to translate particular learning to new
problems. But the overtones were decidedly practical rather than
theoretical or fundamental.

Advertising the practical is likely not only to attract students
who are intent on vocational training but to encourage the faculty

to give the customers what they want. The character and atmosphere of the college are in large part the reflection of the quality and the *motivation* of its students.

The Future of the Liberal Arts College

McGrath and Russell declared that "the divorce of liberal and professional education has been an immense educational and social blunder," and that the liberal arts college of the future will be one which combines general, liberal studies with specialized instruction related to particular occupations.[20] I do not believe that this is the wave of the future in liberal education, even if it be the projection of a historical curve. I readily concede society's need for technical and semiprofessional training in the community two-year college, for a wide range of vocational curricula in state colleges, and for many kinds of professional programs in the universities, although I would be much happier about these institutions if all of them recognized the centrality of liberal studies, instead of making general and liberal education incidental to specialized vocational instruction. But I submit that the future of the elite colleges and of the relatively strong independent liberal arts colleges is not to model themselves on the multipurpose institutions, but to devote themselves wholeheartedly and distinctively to the liberation of intelligence, the dissipation of prejudice, the cultivation of sensibilities, and the active interest in ideas which characterize the thoughtful and sensitive, the truly educated man.

McGrath and Russell contend that it is psychologically and socially sound to combine liberal and professional education. I doubt, however, that the professed liberal arts colleges which have added such curricula as recreation, medical technology, nursing, accounting, retailing, occupational therapy, and radio speech over the years have done so for compelling philosophical reasons. What they did, I suspect, was to hedge their bets on liberal education by trying to compete for students with the public institutions that offered a growing array of vocational courses. Perhaps it was once necessary to adulterate the college program to get enough students to keep even good colleges afloat, but I am confident that the way

[20] McGrath and Russell, *op. cit.*, p. 15.

for good liberal arts colleges to become better ones is to put aside the irrelevances of the collegiate culture, to prune their vocational digressions, and to turn themselves into intellectual communities.

DISCUSSION OF RECENT RESEARCH

ALLEN D. BRECK (*Professor of History, University of Denver*): Dr. McConnell, what specific steps can be taken to improve the quality of education in a university college of liberal arts which has among its faculty members a large number of professionally oriented persons who consistently vote against measures designed to upgrade general education?

DR. MCCONNELL: I don't think there is any easy solution to this problem. Obviously, part of the solution involves the initial selection of broadly educated professional people and the appointment of administrative officers who can exercise some degree of leadership and, if need be, some degree of control. If the faculty of a school of business administration believes that most of the student's undergraduate program should consist of specialized courses in business administration and if it gets its own way, the liberal arts faculty is up against it and, perhaps, should be up against it. This situation can get way out of hand. I can cite, for example, a state college which offers only the master's degree and has far more courses in business administration than a university which awards the doctorate.

Another approach to this problem, of course, is to engage the faculty in a serious study of the purposes of liberal education, the aims of a university, and the basic requirements of professional education. In some institutions, professional education is being broadened and liberalized to the great benefit of professional practice. I have in mind the medical school programs at the University of Florida and Western Reserve University, as well as the experimental program which will be undertaken at Northwestern University in the fall of 1961. Wherever faculties have seriously examined the relationship of the professional school to the university, they have concluded that professional education should be securely anchored to the fundamental disciplines and not allowed to drift out of the main stream of the university.

There are also organizational matters that ought to be considered in this connection. For example, at Berkeley, we have a School of Chemistry. To my mind, it is undesirable to have an undergraduate professional school. It should be a department of the college of liberal arts. When I was at the University of Minnesota, I was opposed to the organization of professional schools of arts and music at the undergraduate level for the same reason. These are liberal arts and ought to be treated as such. There are legitimate places for professional schools but not at the undergraduate level. I am inclined to believe that many of the professional schools that we now have at the undergraduate level ought to be shifted to the graduate level, making way for basic education in the liberal arts.

These are some of the things that can be done to solve the problem you described, but I am sure it will not be easy to do any of them. A kind of eternal vigilance is necessary if professional education is to be truly "of the university" as well as "in the university."

NICHOLAS C. BROWN (*Staff Associate, American Council on Education*): Dr. McConnell, to what extent is the vocational emphasis in the college curriculum the result of deliberate internal decision and to what extent is it the result of acquiescence to external pressures exerted upon the college by professional schools through their entrance requirements and by professional societies through their licensing examinations? Aren't predental, premedical, and pre-engineering programs, in particular, determined to some degree by forces outside the college?

DR. McCONNELL: They are, to some degree, of course. I was unhappy when an association was organized for the accreditation of journalism schools, for I knew what would happen. More specialties are being offered in schools of journalism even at the undergraduate level; moreover, courses have proliferated within these specialties because institutions are now accredited by specialties.

Obviously, there are all kinds of outside pressures, especially on public institutions. The University of California has a curriculum on enology—wine making to you. Although practically no students are enrolled in it, the wine industry succeeded in getting a second curriculum established at Fresno State College. Neither institution has enough students to make a program.

I can cite example after example of this sort of outside pressure. But professors are also responsible for professionalization and course proliferation not only in professional schools but also in colleges of liberal arts. Recently, in helping to survey a liberal arts college which has a good reputation, I found as many as 125 credits being offered in a single department. This is the kind of thing that McGrath has documented on a much larger scale. Professors sometimes expand their offerings until they distort a liberal arts college from a compact, reasonably defined institution into a formless institution of miscellaneous courses and credits. I think all of these forces contribute to the trend toward the vocational college culture.

LEILA A. SUSSMANN (*Assistant Professor, Department of Sociology and Anthropology, Wellesley College*): Last evening, President Gross made a very important point when he said that, if we want to introduce freshmen to the intellectual life of the college, we have to make sure first that there is already a genuine intellectual life on the campus. If there is an intellectual life already in existence, we can be pretty sure that the upperclassmen will introduce the freshmen to it.

This morning, Professor Sanford stated that, if there is a strong anti-intellectual element pervading the campus culture, the faculty has to intervene somehow before the upperclassmen "orient" the freshmen. What I want to know is this: By what specific devices and arrangements can the faculty come to have a decisive influence on the entering student and thus begin to "turn the tide" on such a campus?

PROFESSOR SANFORD: That is a key question, and I do want to underscore what I said about the crucial role of the faculty in this matter.

Of course, I suppose we could change the campus climate by changing the admissions policy, that is to say, by going out and getting students who are not only bright in the usual sense but also "intellectual." However, even if we did this successfully, we could not ignore the strategic role of the faculty.

We must make changes in the freshman curriculum and the way it is taught so that freshmen are brought into much closer association with the faculty. By this, I don't mean that faculty members should be nursemaids to the freshmen. The amount of time faculty members spend with students is of much less importance than the *quality* of their contacts. If we put our minds to it, I am confident that we can devise many arrangements through which the faculty can exert greater influence on entering students.

First of all, we must take full advantage of opportunities for informal and semiformal contacts. A good conversation in the campus hangout following an evening concert might be a much more important contact than any number of formal faculty-student conferences.

Second, without exploiting the faculty too much, we must reorganize regular teaching schedules to provide variations to the endless lectures. I think we undertake to teach too much. We are hypnotized by this notion that there is a specific body of knowledge everyone must learn. Since it can be demonstrated that two years later nobody remembers very much of what he learned in college, we should concentrate more on training the student's intelligence and encouraging his natural interests. For example, instead of giving three lectures a week to a class of forty students, a teacher might occasionally give one lecture and then have his colleagues help him hold small discussion groups during the rest of the week. However it is done (and it need not be expensive), we must create a variety of new situations in which the faculty can associate with students and, thereby, significantly increase its influence.

DR. SUSSMANN: Dr. McConnell, I have been wondering whether the Center for the Study of Higher Education has trained its sights on those few colleges in which the faculty does seem to create a very favorable climate for intellectual activity and, if so, whether you and your colleagues have discovered the formula for the magic that takes place there.

DR. McCONNELL: The center isn't doing exactly what you suggest; however, it is intensively studying students' initial characteristics and the changes that occur during the ensuing four years. This is being done at Reed, Swarthmore, Antioch, and San Francisco State College and to some extent at St. Olaf College, the College of the Pacific, the University of Portland, and the University of California at Berkeley. One of the reasons for choosing colleges like Reed, Antioch, and Swarthmore is that over the years these colleges have sent on to graduate schools a relatively large percentage of students with high intellectual motivation.

When he was at the University of Minnesota helping us plan these studies, Dr. John G. Darley, now executive secretary of the American Psychological Association, suggested that it is not what certain colleges do but the students to whom they do it that accounts for their unusual productivity. Dr. John Holland has made essentially the same point in one of his studies. The colleges that have the highest records of productivity attract National Merit Scholarship winners who are more able, according to scholastic aptitude scores, than National Merit Scholarship students who go to less productive colleges. We are about to publish an article in *Science,* indicating that more able students, according to scholastic aptitude scores, go to the productive institutions and that the students who go to these colleges have an unusually high interest in ideas as ideas, rather than in their practical consequences. In comparison to students who go to less productive colleges, these students score very high on measures of theoretical and esthetic orientation and on measures of ambiguity and flexibility.

Nevertheless, we are not proceeding on the assumption that it is only the students and not the faculty or campus climate that accounts for the eminence of these highly productive colleges. As a matter of fact, we strongly suspect that it is a fortunate conjunction of student characteristics, faculty interests and expectations, and institutional climate that makes a particular college distinctive.

DR. STERN: I should like to add a brief comment to what Dr. McConnell has just said about the relationship between students and their environments.

At Syracuse, we have been studying this specific relationship in a large number of institutions. When we examined student characteristics, we found two contrasting variables: an interest in academic achievement on the one hand, and an interest in heterosexual social activities on the other. We also discovered, however, that students having either one of these specific interests are not found in any one specific kind of institution. Conversely, we discovered that institutions which seem to stress either academic achievement or heterosexual social activity do not necessarily attract students with just these corresponding dominant interests. If our sample is at all typical, academic and social interests are *diffused* through all the student bodies; they are not neatly sorted out.

On the other hand, we do find that schools which stress academic achievement have a specific type of student body consisting of students who tend, in general, to have a broad intellectual interest in science and the humanities but reject social activities and other things of this nature. Conversely, those schools which are described as having a high heterosexual emphasis have students who describe their own interests in terms of a high degree of personal aggression, a high degree of dominance, a high degree of fantasied achievement, a low degree of deference, and a low degree of abasement.

It may well be that where the peer culture takes over, where dating is the important thing, the only way for a student to survive is to be an aggressive youngster with lots of fantasied achievements.

ROBERT E. L. STRIDER (*President, Colby College*): I am interested in Dr. Goldsen's final question, which she left unanswered. I think we could profitably discuss the senior's feeling that his college experience has not fulfilled all his hopes and expectations. I suspect that part of his disappointment is with himself. His human proneness to inertia and his natural susceptibility to certain campus attitudes have kept him from taking full advantage of all the opportunities that were open to him. However, when a senior says, "What a fool I was not to have worked harder and not to have done this or that," I also suspect that his vaccination has taken, and I take some comfort in this.

DR. GOLDSEN: Even though President Strider's statement doesn't require an answer, I want to make a comment. Like the senior he describes, we have not been bold enough ourselves; we have not seized our advantages and exploited our opportunities with sufficient faith and zeal.

As a sociologist, I should like to remind you of something. One of the dominant beliefs of the American people is that education is a good thing. There is genuine consensus on this. Our 1,800 colleges and universities are eloquent testimony to this belief; moreover, they are probably the last strongholds in American life where practical and economic considerations are expected to yield to intellectual considerations. This situation gives us a much greater latitude for being bold than we take advantage of. For some reason, we seem hesitant about using it.

Now, harking back to the discussion last night, I want to make a comment about the relationship between "drudgery" and excellence as it also applies to our hesitancy and lack of boldness. What is a college education supposed to be? Entertainment? Recall President Gross's remark about the choral society. Those of you who have sung in such a group know that there is much drudgery connected with excellence in music—endless repetitions of just one phrase and the like. At first, it is more like drudgery than entertainment.

Curiously enough, students accept drudgery when someone is bold enough to make them see that it is a pathway to excellence. Look at the football team. The coach doesn't entertain the members of the team. He demands strenuous effort that resembles drudgery more than entertainment. Good performance is both their incentive and their reward. So should it be in everything else. Mastery of a foreign language cannot be acquired painlessly; competence in mathematics is not achieved without effort; and effectiveness in the fine arts is not developed without discipline.

The professional athlete, linguist, mathematician, musician, and artist have a way of making their performances look easy. Perhaps this is one mark of a professional. If so, it is very misleading to the unsophisticated student. The beautifully effortless performance of a figure skating champion tends to persuade all of us that we can do the same things. That is precisely why it is excellent. But think of the effort that went into achieving the effortless appearance!

What saves these efforts from being drudgery? *The shared assumption that this effort is essential to reach a worthy aim and the shared desire to reach a genuine standard of excellence.* Only this assumption and this desire will sustain a student until he gets over the hump. There comes a point in the study of language, music, and mathematics when everything begins to fall into place, when all the previous work suddenly pays off, when new possibilities are seen for the first time, and when the subject comes alive. Too many students never get over the hump. I suppose this is why former President Conant of Harvard has said that taking two years of a foreign language is like drilling for oil and stopping just short of a strike!

If we are going to be diffident about the effort that must be invested and feel that we must entertain students in order to make up for it, then we shall not succeed in conveying the spark that President Gross spoke of.

I think we ought to keep in mind throughout this conference these two points: First, campuses are the last stronghold where it can be demonstrated not only that education is a good thing but also that the intellectual life is important and exciting. Second, we should state boldly that the rewards of the intellectual life are worth working for. I think we should not be so deferential or diffident about acknowledging this fact. Falling in love with a subject transforms drudgery into something that is no longer drudgery. The romance of learning is worth the work it involves. One just does it. And he is saved by the spark, not by the entertainment.

JOSEPH A. SELLINGER, S.J. (*Dean, College of Arts and Sciences, Georgetown University*): How do we convince freshmen that the drudgery they must go through is drudgery not for the sake of drudgery, but for the sake of learning?

DR. GOLDSEN: The problem isn't the same for all departments. In engineering, for example, almost the whole curriculum is slide rule drill and laboratory practice. Here the students know that this is a necessary part of a total pattern; they can see it clearly, and they accept it.

In English, sociology, psychology, and other disciplines, the problem of engaging the student is somewhat different. Here we tend to be more apologetic about the drudgery involved because the aims are less practical and because, in the minds of the students, the rewards are less tangible. For this very reason, we have to demonstrate our conviction that the values we seek are worth the price that must be paid. We have to be as tough as the football coach.

FATHER SELLINGER: This is exactly what the freshmen resist. They don't see where the drudgery is taking them. The professor says, "We are teaching this because you will need it and appreciate it later on." For most students, this is not convincing enough.

DR. GOLDSEN: As President Gross said last night, it is just like a love affair. It is not the words; it is the music. A person can say, "I love you," but it is not convincing. It is the exchange of spiritual stuff that convinces even in the absence of words. Right?

Well, I think that is the answer. When a freshman comes to a university, sits in a mathematics class, and sees a real pro, he senses something deeper than words can convey. The professor may seem dull; he may grind it out; he may even do a Bob Benchley on the blackboard. Then one day the freshman sees a little drama that he does not soon forget. He sees the professor tackle a new problem, momentarily forget the class, throw himself into it, strike a snag, revise his strategy, get control of the problem, and finally solve it. He also sees an unvarnished enthusiasm and an unexpressed satisfaction that he will remember long after he has forgotten the solution. This is one of the most rewarding experiences the student can expect to get out of college, and he somehow knows it.

The other day in one of my classes a girl came to me and said, "I couldn't sleep all night because of what you said the other day," and she wanted to go on. I threw my arms around her and said, "Honey, I love you." If I can make a student stay awake, I think that is pretty good, don't you?

ALAN SIMPSON (*Dean of the College, University of Chicago*): Since I am very much a newcomer to this whole business, I wonder if I could ask Professor Sanford to give us a rapid evaluation of research on the college student. As I have listened to various reports, I have found that some of the observations correspond to my own and some do not. Obviously, these studies have been more systematic than any casual observations I have made; therefore, it would be helpful to me if he would explain the two or three most important lessons from this research that were unknown to us before the research was conducted.

PROFESSOR SANFORD: This reminds me of the typical response to the research at Vassar. I think the typical faculty opinion was that our results fell into two classes: (*a*) things that were not true and (*b*) things that were true but that everyone knew already.

Seriously, I do not think that research on the college student can be evaluated this simply, and I am certainly not in a position to single out the major results for anyone except myself.

For me, one of the most important results has been the evidence that personality can and does develop during the college years. We are beginning to learn something now about the circumstances that make a difference in personality development; however, the discussion we have just had about discipline and drudgery illustrates to me how much more we need to learn. I think that we should be much more careful about our generalizations than we have been so far.

There is a grimness that pervades many college campuses today. Many faculty members have the notion that the way to deal with the nonintellectual and anti-intellectual trends among the students is to give them more work. I do not think that this "get tough" policy is really conducive either to the creation of an intellectual atmosphere or to the development of individual personality.

When discipline is imposed upon an individual without regard to his own purpose and without his acceptance of the other person's purpose, it leads to an authoritarianism which itself is anti-intellectual. As we know from examining students in engineering schools, if we enforce discipline which a student really doesn't accept and cannot connect with his own purposes, we really just reinforce the unquestioning conformity that he acquired in high school and that he should abandon in college.

The football coach can "pour it on" because he knows the students share his purpose. They *want* to be made to do what he asks; they *want* to be made to do their best in the interest of the common purpose. But it is very difficult to use this model in the classroom, where students are encouraged to compete with each other. We cannot expect to create a group spirit in the classroom as we do on the athletic field. In the classroom the teacher must create quite a different relationship. He must persuade the student that there is an adult who knows what he can do, who cares about what he can do, and who, therefore, is in a position to make meaningful demands upon him.

It is all very well for teachers to demand a lot of students, but these demands are self-defeating unless the student knows that they are really designed to bring out the best in him and not to perpetuate some set of values that he doesn't yet share. All this follows from the theory of development. Our biggest task is to develop this theory so that we really know what we are doing and how we can relate what we are doing to a clear conception of what actually makes a difference in the development of students. For me the most important thing that has come out of our research is an improved conception of what personality development is and how we might bring it about.

Naturally, I am glad if these results accord with what knowledgeable educators have known all along about student development. Scientific work is bound to repeat and reaffirm common-sense notions, but it often sheds new light that enables us to go beyond common-sense conceptions. This matter of discipline is a case in point.

I think it is very fine to talk about the romance of learning, but I am not sure what this really means in psychological terms. Here is a student who is what he is, and here is a curriculum. What actually happens when the student "falls in love" with learning? This is all quite vague as it has been put to us so far because no one has composed a psychological theory in which the elements of this process are clear and understandable.

I think we have maneuvered ourselves into a very awkward position by talking about the romance of learning when the whole atmosphere of the college is most unromantic. Nobody has been heard to laugh aloud in the faculty club at Berkeley for years and years. Maybe that is because there is no intellectual life there. At lunch, the professors talk about departmental politics or about esoteric matters that they can't share with anybody except their colleagues in the same narrow specialty.

This activity is not intellectual, and it is not a model for students who are going to become intellectual. My experience with faculties is that we don't talk about intellectual matters. If we are not talking about departmental affairs or highly esoteric matters, there is desultory conversation about the political campaign or something of that kind. So I think it ill becomes faculty members to talk about discipline when the discipline is really not in the interest of developing truly intellectual attitudes in students.

POINTS OF VIEW

What are the essential factors involved in successfully
introducing entering students to the intellectual life of
the college?

What are the implications of these factors for the student,
faculty member, counselor, and administrator?

STUDENT: TIMOTHY JENKINS, *National Affairs Vice-President,
United States National Student Association*

FACULTY MEMBER: AARON SAYVETZ, *Professor of the Physical Sciences in
the College, University of Chicago*

COUNSELOR: ARTHUR A. HITCHCOCK, *Executive Director, American Personnel and Guidance Association*

ADMINISTRATOR: ALAN SIMPSON, *Dean of the College, University of
Chicago*

TIMOTHY JENKINS—STUDENT

At first, I thought it was a burst of academic generosity on the
part of the American Council to allow the student to speak before
the faculty member, the counselor, and the dean; however, I've
had a second thought about this. In "bringing up the rear" the
dean has the opportunity to present a total refutation! Since the
dean will have the last word, I am not at all sure now whether
it is an advantage or a disadvantage to appear first!

I suppose there are two ways of examining the essential factors
involved in introducing the entering student to the intellectual
life of the college. One could take either a descriptive or a normative approach to the subject, but both approaches have certain
defects. If one merely lists current practices, he does not come to

85

grips with the basic issue of whether or not they are effective; if he proposes a plan of his own, he runs the risk of basing it on his own relatively narrow personal experience. So, in an effort to avoid both defects and still preserve both advantages, let me begin descriptively and conclude normatively so that my recommendations can be based on observations that are wider than my own experience.

I think it is significant that representatives of American higher education should meet here to discuss methods of transmitting intellectual values to its initiates who, in time, determine the character it assumes. I suppose the crux of our concern is that we not merely bring the freshman to college but really bring the college to the freshman.

This morning, we had a review of various studies of the student's background and environment and an analysis of how these factors relate to his achievement in college. I think that careful study would likewise show that orientation practices also have a demonstrable influence on his later adjustment. We might find it valuable, therefore, to survey some of the common procedures employed to orient freshmen to campus life. In most instances, orientation to college consists of a four- to eight-day period when freshmen are welcomed and welcomed again by administrative and student government personnel. In addition, they are subjected to batteries of achievement and aptitude tests, physically examined, psychologically catalogued, and systematically bathed in the language of abstract educational platitude, not without some specific references to their particular institution's noble traditions. Finally, they are assured that they are the salt of the earth and that they will probably excel any previous class in scholastic achievement and professional endeavor.

But one of the component parts of the academic community is almost always excluded from participation in this elaborate procedure. The faculty is conspicuous by its absence. If one wants to verify this startling fact, he need only consult a collection of freshman handbooks and see for himself the general plan which orientation programs characteristically follow. The administrators, the chaplains, the counselors, the ROTC personnel, and the student leaders all speak, but scarcely ever is the professor introduced as an essential part of this new life.

Now that we have mentioned it, let us go further into the freshman handbook, remembering that it is shoved under the nose of the freshman as his new "bible" of campus norms. We find in its "sacred" pages all sorts of epigrammatic messages and exhortations, photographs of all of the extracurricular bigwigs, a complete dictionary of campus "slanguage," a calendar of upcoming social events along with a "run down" of the Panhellenic utopia, and, last but not least, a list of the particular obeisances to be paid to upperclassmen whenever a freshman is so unfortunate as to encounter one of these exalted creatures in the course of his humble educational quest during that first semester.

It is significant to note that eight out of ten of these pamphlets emphasize the light side of college life and heap prestige on the nonacademic areas of student life. Honor societies, if mentioned at all, are seldom given more than a listing, and, under no circumstances, are their presidents afforded the privilege of addressing the freshmen. This privilege is reserved only for their fun-oriented Greek counterparts.

Why am I so aggressive in my remarks about the practices of this week-long orientation? Why do I make light of the time-honored tradition of freshman handbooks? Well, for one thing, I am disturbed when I try to estimate realistically the amount of harm done in this relatively short period through this series of apparently innocuous orientation rituals. Dana Farnsworth states in *Mental Health in College and University:*

. . . incoming freshmen are always aware that the road to status in the college community is social, not intellectual, if not administrative rather than educational. . . . in their quest for status they adopt those values necessary for achievement and in turn pass that tradition on to the subsequent classes. In this manner, an unbroken chain of values is established in which intellectual traits are definitely subordinate.[1]

I am convinced that this situation can be remedied only with the cooperation of *student leaders,* faculty, and administration.

[1] Farnsworth, *Mental Health in College and University* (Cambridge, Mass.: Harvard University Press, 1957).

I say this with emphasis because some of the comments this morning suggested that the administrator or the faculty member can
control the intellectual climate. I feel very strongly that the intellectual aura of an institution is determined, in the final analysis,
by the students themselves.

Freshmen do not want to be welcomed a dozen times to their
college. Young minds will be attracted to learning if the planning
committee will take the trouble to see to it that someone says
something intellectually stimulating. Faculty members, as well as
outstanding students, should be allowed to participate as equals in
college orientation programs. During the first months of college,
the most exotic creatures in the freshman's world are the members
of the faculty and the honor student. These important groups
should no longer be ignored.

I think it would be naïve to expect intellectual orientation of a
real sort to take place in only a week, for this is the basic purpose
of the whole college program. It is reasonable, however, to expect
this one week to set the stage for intellectual work and not to run
counter to it. I am not debunking extracurricular activity; I am
just stressing the need for sensible balance.

Before classes begin, it might be valuable to have workshops in
which freshmen could be exposed to certain concepts such as academic freedom, the aims of a university, and the like. Informal
discussions on other important topics could be arranged throughout the year, particularly during the off hours in the freshman
dormitories. Faculty members and administrators could be drawn
into these small circles so that the freshmen could get a more
complete picture of college life. If we thought in terms of a year
instead of a week, we could also develop a series of freshmen
lectures without compulsory attendance after its first few sessions.
In addition to its own resources, the college could use visiting
speakers to add sparkle to such a program.

I suppose what I am proposing here is not just an improvement
of orientation but also an improvement of the intellectual life in
general. The main thing is that we should make sure that freshmen
are a part of that life from the very beginning so that they will see
the teacher and the honor student as important figures in their
lives. I think this is possible, and I think this is the method that

we are all suggesting when we talk about the "romance of learn-ing," but I would prefer to call it "a way of life."

We are looking for an effective transition between high school and college, a significant change when the teacher becomes a scholar-learner, when the homework assignment becomes inde-pendent study, and when the examination becomes an opportunity for expression, assessment, and further discussion. We are looking for an environment in which the faculty, students, and adminis-trators both individually and collectively are interested primarily in learning, an environment in which learning is a way of life and permeates the very air.

Finally, we must recognize, as Plato did, that true education leads man eventually to contemplate the good and the beautiful in all its manifestations, not merely to speak about them as ideals but to seek them actively as a way of life. It is this spirit that warms the intellectual climate, that gives purpose to the search for truth, and that attracts young minds and hearts to the whole great enterprise.

AARON SAYVETZ—FACULTY MEMBER

Although I am here to discuss the problem before us from the viewpoint of the faculty member, I hasten to say that I am speak-ing for myself. Anyone who has ever attended a faculty meeting knows that it is not only unrealistic and imprudent to speak for the faculty generally, it is inconceivable.

What are the essential factors involved in successfully introduc-ing entering students to the intellectual life of the college? One factor is that there be an intellectual life in evidence, one in which students already on the campus are actively and obviously engaged. For it is students, I think, who transmit to one another in an immediate way the facts of life—I mean the facts of academic life. If there are discrepancies between the high-sounding speeches of orientation and the attitudes and standards that actually prevail, the truth will out. The critical point, therefore, is not so much what happens in orientation week, important as it is, but what has been happening for years before. Where the student body has become committed to the educational aims of the college because it understands them, where the physical organization of living permits the student to work toward those aims, and where the social organization of student life encourages their achievement rather than the opposite, the initiation of entering students is likely to be successful. Contrariwise, the most inspired faculty will have difficulty reaching its freshman over the inert mass of an indifferent student body. All this means that the best guarantee for the continuation of an active intellectual life on the campus is an active intellectual life on the campus.

At bottom, of course, the faculty bears the primary responsibility. There is first the essential fact (I hope it is a fact) of the individual faculty member's intellectual life. This is, as the mathematicians say, a necessary condition. But is it a sufficient one? We know that the public reputation of a productive faculty enhances the prestige of a college or university and may, for one thing, attract numbers of students who are already impressively intellectual. Furthermore, students are likely to be strongly motivated by association with distinguished professors. This is all to the good, but it may mean little to the development of the student's own intellectual life unless the characteristic modes of analysis and synthesis, the means by which knowledge is achieved as well as the end product, are exhibited and taught day by day and week by week. The distinction here is between the student's getting a sun tan in the reflected glow of the professor's glory and the student's active involvement in the intellectual enterprise, between the passive audience and the active participant. There are ways of teaching and choices of curricular materials which favor the one or the other. I think, for example, that where the scholarly oration or lecture is too heavily relied upon, passivity is promoted. Where the classroom is more like a forum and less like a platform, where there can be both action and reaction, the student can get some intellectual exercise on the spot.

But the individual faculty member in his individual classroom is only part of the picture. Our topic has been phrased in terms of the intellectual life of the college, which for me connotes the possibility of a total greater than the sum of its parts. I mean the curriculum as a whole. The term once meant a racecourse, and so it is regarded, unfortunately, by some students who speed toward a pot of gold or matrimony at the finish line. The dictionaries put it as the totality of courses listed in the catalogue, or perhaps that collection required of the student. These meanings, while all too true, are no more satisfactory for our purpose than the ancient Roman one. The question is: Can the formal intellectual life of the college, as embodied in the curriculum offered to an individual student, be made intelligible to him? Can it be defended as a basis for the intellectual life of the student, not only while he is on the campus but also after he has left it? Does it have a rationale dictated by this function? Or—to put the alternative in an extreme form—is it a hodgepodge?

I believe that faculties must give continuing thought to the form and substance of a curriculum that can fulfill this purpose. An institution whose faculty participates in the creation and sustenance of a coherent curriculum is in a favorable position to introduce entering students to the formal intellectual life of the college because (*a*) the form of its intellectual life is likely to be intelligible and can therefore be communicated, and (*b*) the effort of each faculty member is reinforced by the efforts of all and by the understanding of the student body.

ARTHUR A. HITCHCOCK—Counselor

The counselor is concerned with the individual student. This is important to keep in mind because at this conference we have naturally had to think in terms of groups of students, such as those in the classroom. In considering the work of the counselor in connection with academic or intellectual orientation, however, we must think of the student as an individual. This, I feel, is a most important distinction.

A problem that continually confronts counselors is that they are always dealing with information about groups. Thus, when a counselor talks with a student about the significance of a particular test score, he usually interprets it in terms of averages or norms of a large group of test scores. Although a counselor must know a great deal about groups, he must constantly and consciously keep in mind the fact that this information is only general background for his work with the individual student. Although he must be familiar with the interpretation of the group norms and the institutional setting, he must focus on the individual.

Today's college freshman comes from a high school in which he probably has had, thanks to the National Defense Education Act, a certain amount of counseling. Although much of this counseling has been good, some of it has undoubtedly been rather poor. For example, Paul Heist discovered that a group of counselors in California had no idea of the identity of the top-ranking academic institutions in that state and that their knowledge of the characteristics of other institutions was equally faulty. I can say this about counselors because I am identified with them.

Although there are some promising developments taking place in high school counseling, college people must bear in mind that high school counselors often work under certain restrictions. For example, many students come to college with rather limited horizons and frequently with quite unrealistic career plans. Also, high school students frequently lack models that we would like them to have at this period of their lives. These conditions make it all the more important for the college to see that the freshman gets a new conception of himself and that he is exposed to challenging models of what he might become.

The college counselor can be exceedingly helpful to the freshman who is making the crucial transition from high school to college with all its mental and emotional adjustments. In picking up the student as he comes from high school, the college counselor should give very serious thought to the problem of attrition in the freshman year. The attrition at the freshman level is still so heavy that one often wonders whether any real wisdom is involved in the selection of a college on the part of many students. This is a most serious matter, as the dropout statistics show. In an excellent article on the "cooling-out process," Dr. McConnell's colleagues show that a good student frequently enters the wrong kind of institution, becomes discouraged, and discontinues his education prematurely. With wise counseling, such a student can often be encouraged to continue his studies in another institution that provides a climate and program more congenial to his interests and abilities.

What I have tried to say thus far is that the role of the counselor is an important one in orienting the student to the intellectual life of the college and in determining whether or not the able but misplaced student has any college experience at all.

To be effective, the professional college counselor should be broadly educated, well trained in his field, and, ideally, have a Ph.D. in counseling psychology or a related discipline. In addition, he should have the ability to work effectively with individual students, faculty members, and administrators. Finally, he should be intimately acquainted with the characteristics and climate of his own institution.

In a study presented yesterday at another meeting in Princeton, it was pointed out that a high school counselor does not appear to earn his salt for about three years. This may be even more true of the college counselor, for it naturally takes some time to become acquainted with the unique characteristics of any institution. The counselor must know what the academic demands are; likewise, he must know what attitudes and practices militate against intellectual achievement at his own institution.

There is evidence, for example, that in some of our institutions particular departments are hostile to the career development of women. Here, then, is a situation in which the counselor has to be fully aware of what the attitudes are and what their effect is on the individual student. In this instance he should understand, too, something about the whole problem of the career development of girls, particularly as it applies to this situation when the student is at a very formative stage.

The college counselor needs to know not only the things that one can generally learn from tests and other devices but also the things that a perceptive person can learn directly from the student himself. He must then help the student to understand himself, to know his own abilities and limitations, and to formulate general aims that are appropriate to his interests and talents. In doing all this, however, the counselor must be aware of his own natural biases and be careful not to let these intrude at the wrong time.

There have been times, I am sure, when counselors have tended in clinical settings to remake students according to their own models, which sometimes have been those of the socially adept person or the big-man-on-the-campus. Whatever his biases are, the counselor must be especially careful not to inflict them unthinkingly upon a student.

Finally, the college counselor must have close relationships with faculty members and must be fully aware of the idiosyncracies of various departments. He cannot work effectively with a student unless he knows these things. Knowing them, he can be of great help to both the student and the department.

A really good counselor can contribute a great deal to the development of the intellectual climate of the college. To do so, however, he must himself be intellectually oriented; he must understand the inner workings of the institution; and he must have close relationships with the individual student, the faculty members, and the administrators.

ALAN SIMPSON—Administrator

The "essential factors" have become clear enough: We need a student body that is capable of an intellectual life, a college that has one to offer, and some arrangements for a happy marriage.

As I listen to many of the worries that have been expressed here, I find myself in a somewhat peculiar position. The College at Chicago has its problems, but they are not in this area. It is not primarily a mating institution; it is not a finishing school or a vocational school; it is not a passport into a bank or a brokerage house; it is not a holding operation for a football team. If there are light-minded students who are sauntering through its halls or playing poker on their beds, the standards are set by sterner spirits. There are no more jealous guardians of the intellectual life than our student leaders.

So my problem is not to establish a tradition but to maintain its quality, to broaden its range, and to warn a few earnest souls that they are in danger of becoming prigs or bores if they take themselves too seriously.

As the dean of such an institution, I have to watch the proportions of any activity that might threaten the good things we enjoy. From time to time an alumnus urges us to restore football. What would be wrong with a little football? At Chicago, we know how inevitably the little football would become a big football. We also have certain reserves about fraternities. We enjoy them as one component in our pluralistic life, but we would not be interested in seeing them dominate the campus.

I have to uphold the ideal of a vigorous general education in the face of the pressures of vocationalism and specialization. Vocationalism, in some of the forms discussed here, is not a problem; however, anyone who has tried to organize a liberal education within a research institution knows that there are perils as well as privileges in that setting. A healthy intellectual life for the undergraduate depends on his exposure to a wide range of ideas outside his major, and limits must be set to the claims of professional studies.

I have to concern myself with the tone of classroom teaching. If undergraduates are left to the mercies of graduate assistants, if the campus celebrity is heard only at a distance, if ideas are smothered in facts, if the outrageous hypothesis is rarely broached, if the rebel is looked at askance, in short, if the atmosphere breeds a dull docility, the richest orientation program is not going to conceal the poverty of the institution.

I have to see that the right furnishings for an intellectual life are provided outside the classroom. How often does a campus bookstore in America provide the education of a Blackwell's? Why have we allowed the ideal of a residential college to deteriorate, in the course of its westward migration, into a mindless motel? How can we provide in our different situations for the right sort of contacts between students and faculty or between students and visitors, who can infect them with their own sense of standards?

If by these and other steps we can nourish an intellectual life, it ought to be easy enough to introduce an interested student to it. No British university, to my knowledge, bothers with an orientation program—if we except a few remarks and introductions on the opening day. In terms of our particular interest, British educators would say that the evidences of an intellectual life are either there or they are not there. If they are there, the students who are going to benefit from them will have their imaginations seized soon enough.

At Chicago, our orientation program must be one of the longest in the nation—a prodigious battery of placement tests; a variety of talks and discussions; a retreat into the country for relaxation and more talk while the placement results are worked out; an explicit effort by administrators, faculty, and older students to explain what education is about. We consider this a necessary and, on the whole, successful introduction, but the real test is what follows.

DISCUSSION

Presiding: S. TOWN STEPHENSON, *Dean of the Faculty, Washington State University; Member, Commission on the College Student*

Chairman Stephenson: There we have it, the viewpoints of a student, a faculty member, a counselor, and an administrator. I think that we should not attempt to decide which one is the most influential in establishing an intellectual climate, for, obviously, all of them have vital and strategic roles in this undertaking.

It seems clear, too, that we should not attempt to define "the best orientation program." Institutions have tremendous differences, and the intellectual life will be encouraged differently on different campuses in accordance with the particular institution's aims, its faculty's interests, and its students' characteristics. What we *do* want to identify clearly, though, are some of the essential factors that are involved in this whole process.

As Mr. Jenkins pointed out, we cannot hope to bring about a complete orientation to the intellectual life of the college in one week, nor can we do it at all if we fail to secure the full support of the students and to involve them in a significant way. To start the discussion, therefore, I should like to ask Mr. Jenkins how we can *effectively* enlist the student in this effort—at least more effectively than in the instances he cited.

MR. JENKINS: One of the presumptions that people seem to make is that students have to be dragged into anything that is intellectually worthwhile, that they are really not concerned enough to participate when they are given an opportunity to do so. I think this initial misconception is the first thing we have to deal with.

If the many campuses I have had a chance to visit are at all representative, there exists almost without exception in every educational community a group of vigorous students who are very much concerned with the serious business of learning. Ofttimes, the intellectual tone of the campus depends upon whether or not this element is in power. But students with intellectual interests do exist on almost every campus. One of the things that has to be done, it seems to me, is to increase their influence, to see that they have an opportunity to bring to the entire campus community all that they have to offer.

I have actually known groups of such students who were unable to get space for informal discussions of the classics, Greek and Roman literature, art, or other special interests. Since they were not organized along conventional lines and did not have "a program," they could not make the necessary impression. Here is where the faculty member could be instrumental in encouraging students with serious interests by giving some of his off-hours time and by requesting the administration to provide modest facilities.

I firmly believe that students with intellectual interests do exist, and I am equally sure that they would exert much greater influence if they were given more encouragement and support.

WILLIAM E. CADBURY, JR. (*Dean, Haverford College*): At Haverford College, the orientation program is organized by students. The administration helps decide only such questions as whether it should involve five or six days and matters of that sort. The students themselves run the program and generally do a good job. The only question that concerns us is the one Mr. Jenkins raised. Are the students who are selected to run the program those who want to project an image of the outstanding student or are they those who want to project an image of the big-man-on-the-campus?

I think orientation programs on most campuses have grown out of the old tradition of hazing freshmen. Hazing was a way of initiating the freshmen into the mores of the institution, and it gradually fell into disrepute. Students of a more responsible turn of mind, probably encouraged by college officials, took over the process of orientation, which has become what we have today. I think this is what happened historically; however, I also think we are still confronted with the same old problem of how to put it and keep it in the hands of responsible students.

MR. MORRISSEY: I should like to raise a mild objection to the faint disparagement I detect here of students who engage in extracurricular activities. I think that we should not discount the educational experience that a student gains from debating, dramatics, music, publications, student government, or some other activity. Reasonable participation in these activities, although they may not be intellectual in the purest sense, does not run counter to serious study. Study and out-of-class activities, far from being uncongenial, often enhance one another. As a matter of fact, the good student is not infrequently a campus leader; yet we speak of the scholar and the BMOC as though they had to be opposite types. I'm sure they are opposites in some instances, but I am also sure there are enough scholar-leaders to make it hazardous to put black or white tags on them.

If certain outside activities were not considered valuable, no students would be attending this conference!

MR. JENKINS: May I comment on the BMOC. This is a much disputed concept, and I suppose any statement one makes has to be carefully qualified. Having sat in the councils of the mighty where some of these students hold sway, however, I am somewhat skeptical of the phrase "a student leader." He is often a person who, by some sort of machination, has captured the seat of power and become the student representative and voice in administrative affairs. He is often a person who smiles and shakes hands, a little politico within his campus world. I say this, having been a student body president myself and having had a number of friends who served in the same capacity; nevertheless, I have great reservations about this type of student and resist the idea of giving him additional power and influence.

Where does a college find responsible students to run an orientation program? I think that question is a crucial one. I think it is a dangerous precedent for administrators to think of the student government leaders as the only representatives of the student body. Ofttimes they are the Hellenic type, the BMOC stereotype, persons to be really wary of. I have yet to see an orientation program placed in the hands of the chairman of Phi Beta Kappa. I have yet to see the honor society come before the students and present its program in a comprehensive manner. In about eight out of ten cases, the process of orientation gives an unbalanced impression of college life because it focuses only on the extracurricular life. All I ask is that the good student be recognized and represented as an important part of the college community. This ought not to be too difficult to achieve.

TERRI GALVIN (*Executive Secretary, Intercollegiate Association of Women Students; Member of the Commission on the College Student*): I think the intellectual viewpoint is gaining strength among students generally. This can be seen in the trend of many student groups to de-emphasize the trivia they have been concerned with in the past and to embark on more meaningful programs that have intellectual substance. The typical big-man-on-the-campus of the past is, I believe, losing out to the serious student in general influence. I think the time is ripe to give the serious student a voice in the orientation of freshmen, as Mr. Jenkins suggests.

PROFESSOR SAYVETZ: Arthur, when you said, with a little too much emphasis, I thought, that the counselor deals with the student as an individual, you didn't mean to imply, did you, that the faculty member does not?

DR. HITCHCOCK: I certainly meant to say, Aaron, that one of the distinctive features of the counseling situation is that it is characterized by an individual, face-to-face relationship. In distinguishing between teachers and counselors, this seems to be one point on which a distinction could be made. A counselor works with a student in a very close individual relationship in contrast to those who work with students in groups, whether the groups are 18 or 350.

Furthermore, the counselor has to view each student *as an individual* when he works with that student to improve academic performance, to solve an emotional problem, to remove a financial worry, or whatever. The things the counselor knows about groups are helpful, but he knows that they may not apply to the student in front of him. Thus, in addition to dealing with the student on an individual basis, the counselor must consciously *think* of the student as an individual.

PROFESSOR SAYVETZ: It seems to me that one of the choices every teacher has is the choice of dealing with students as a group and nothing more or, on the other hand, of dealing with them as individuals who happen also to be part of a group. I simply cannot yield to you the exclusive prerogative of dealing with the student as an individual even though there may be 18 or 350 in the class.

DR. HITCHCOCK: I can agree with you if you grant the difference of the face-to-face relationship that the counselor has.

PROFESSOR SAYVETZ: I don't give you that; I give you only privacy.

DEAN SIMPSON: As an almost total stranger to professional counseling, may I ask how much intellectual life the typical counselor has? The question is not meant to be rude. Frankly, I am not really acquainted with the counseling service at the college level. I have seen it at the high school level, and I am distressed by the professionalization of the function, which takes people right out of their subject fields and robs them of the very kind of interest they should have and would have if they had a personal commitment to a subject.

KATHRYN L. HOPWOOD (*Dean of Students, Hunter College*): Please say that again!

DEAN SIMPSON: I hope Arthur will forgive me if the question seems to have any discourteous implications. My question is, essentially, how specialized a person is the typical counselor? Is he so specialized that he doesn't have any independent intellectual life of his own?

DR. HITCHCOCK: I think we have to look, first of all, at what the education of a counselor should be. He is (or should be) a person with a liberal arts background and basic work in psychology, anthropology, biology, and related disciplines. With this kind of background, he usually goes on to do graduate work in the field of psychology.

In my experience, the college counselor usually is and wants to be identified with the faculty; he often teaches a course in psychology or a related field. Although there is a difference between a teacher who counsels and a counselor who teaches, I do not think the difference is necessarily in the degree to which each is committed to the intellectual life.

CHAIRMAN STEPHENSON: We have time for just one more question.

PRESIDENT ELKINS: I want to direct this question to Dean Simpson. I was very much interested in what you had to say about fraternities in the light of your background and experience at Chicago. I believe I understood you to say that you would not mind if 250 students belong to fraternities but that you would be somewhat alarmed if as many as 500 belong to fraternities. Did you mean to imply that it wouldn't make too much difference if 250 were lost but that it would be much more detrimental if 500 were lost?

DEAN SIMPSON: No, I didn't mean to imply that fraternity members would be lost at all. There was a period in the history of our institution when fraternities withered on the vine and when the administration was delighted to see them withering on the vine. That is not our current feeling. We feel they have a role to play, and we are willing to give them modest help and to preserve them in a minor role. I think we (students, faculty, and administrators) would be worried if our fraternities ever came to set the tone for the whole student body. Whether the critical figure is 500 or 600, I don't know. But our object is to keep them in a minor role.

DEAN BORRESON: That doesn't quite answer the question. The basic question is: Why? Why do you consider fraternities inherently or potentially detrimental to the climate you wish to maintain at Chicago?

DEAN SIMPSON: We just suspect that the intellectual life that we like to foster, with all its informality and vigor, would probably not flourish if the tone of our campus were set by fraternity life.

JEANNE L. NOBLE (*Assistant Professor of Education, New York University*): Is there evidence to support this as a fact? Are not sororities and fraternities, in some cases, taking the lead in establishing more favorable campus climates? I think it would be very easy for a college to find a scapegoat and say, "We don't have an intellectual climate because of sororities and fraternities." But is this actually the reason for its failure?

DEAN SIMPSON: I should be much happier to turn the question back to those of you who represent colleges where fraternities do play a very dominant role. I can appeal only to the collective judgment on my particular campus. We have represented here many colleges where fraternities have played and are playing a large role. Are the administrators or faculty members at those schools completely happy about this situation? If they are and if they share our interest in the intellectual life, we would have to revise our judgment.

THE COLLEGE STUDENT
AND THE IDEA OF LEARNING

ERNEST HAVEMANN
Author

L AST SUMMER, about the time that I was invited to address this
conference, there was a full-page advertisement in the New
York City newspapers that I wanted to call to your attention. I cut
it out to show you, and then, as intellectuals and even would-be
intellectuals like writers will sometimes do, I absent-mindedly
lost it. But let me tell you about it, because it bears most significantly on this subject of ours. The advertisement showed a man
who was obviously an intellectual. I forget whether the photog-
rapher had equipped him with a Phi Beta Kappa key, or a mortar-
board, or horn-rimmed glasses—but at any rate, you could see at a
glance that the man was unusually brainy. Now the ad, strangely
enough, was for a syndicated Sunday comic strip section, and the
headline on the ad said, "Even the intelligentsia read Dick Tracy."

Well, I have no quarrel with the ad. Intellectuals do read the
comic pages—and this is a very important fact.

The intellectual, you see, is the most adaptable person in our
society. Intellectuals can and do have a wide range of interests,
not all of which are by any means intellectual. All of us have
highly intellectual friends who are great devotees of the comics
or of jazz music, bull fighting, contract bridge, golf, modern paint-
ing, detective stories, and primitive art—none of which is really an
intellectual pursuit in any sense of the word. Moreover, intellectuals spend a good part of their days in nonintellectual activities such as cooking meals—which is not an intellectual pursuit
even though you would hardly think so to listen to some gourmets
talk—or rearing children, mowing lawns, and driving their auto-

mobiles to and from work. Indeed many intellectuals earn their living at nonintellectual jobs. I'm thinking here particularly of a number of my friends who happen to be psychologists or sociologists and are certainly intellectuals, yet whose function in society is running prisons, certainly not an intellectual vocation. Or, to cite an example that is perhaps closer to home to many of you, I am not sure that even teaching college freshmen is an intellectual occupation.

The intellectual helps get a lot of the world's nonintellectual work done. Moreover he supports many of the world's nonintellectual industries and nonintellectual entertainments. The favor, alas, is not returned. Indeed, it cannot be returned. The nonintellectual man and the anti-intellectual man cannot cross this dividing line in the opposite direction. They cannot read and understand the books that the intellectual writes. They cannot bring themselves to seek out the intellectual on his own ground and encourage him to talk about the things that really interest him.

When the intellectual and the nonintellectual meet socially, for example at a cocktail party, it is the intellectual who adapts to the situation and who talks about things like the weather and the sports page and the superficial aspects of politics that the others can understand. It is the interests of the nonintellectual—that is to say, the lowest common intellectual denominator—that prevail. The same phenomenon can be observed in our newspapers, our magazines, our television industry, and even to a large extent in our theater. All these mass media are geared, more or less, to the lowbrow, who will not and perhaps cannot make the effort to rise any higher. It is the intellectual who has to adapt, who has to meet our society somewhat more than halfway, in fact more than three-quarters of the way.

In America even more than in most countries, since this land of ours is huge and its people scattered, the intellectual is often a very lonely man. This is true even among you people who work in the universities, and it is far truer about people such as writers. When authors from England and France visit America, they notice this phenomenon first of all and are still talking about it when they leave. Not even in New York or Chicago, and certainly not in Los Angeles, is there anything like the large and cohesive society of intellectuals who meet to discuss their mutual interests in London and Paris. There is doubtless a society of intellectuals here in Princeton. But even this is cut off by a matter of hundreds or even thousands of miles from most other American intellectuals, who, living scattered among hundreds and thousands of American communities both large and small, are forced to spend most of their social lives, if they care to have them, in the company and at the mercy of nonintellectuals.

Well, I do not mean to get us all weeping here about the plight of the intellectual although, truth to tell, I often do think he is a rather lonely and pathetic and unappreciated figure in our society. I have discussed these matters in some detail because I hope to impress upon you what a difficult job you undertake when you try to introduce the new college student—the newcomer to your campus—to intellectuality. You are trying to move against our society's main stream of traffic. You are a lone voice crying out in the wilderness. If you will permit me a few more mixed metaphors, you are a man with a broom trying to sweep back the tide, a girl with a spanish fan trying to blow back the tornado. You are trying to popularize a way of life that most people cannot understand at all, and that even intellectuals spend only a small part of their lives pursuing. You have an absolutely hopeless task, and I could not admire you more. I pray for you and I urge you on. For, although mankind does not know it and perhaps resents it, you are the one hope of mankind.

Let us consider for a moment what the student who arrives on the campus is really like. Let us permit ourselves to dream happy thoughts and assume that all the new arrivals are the offspring of America's finest families, with fathers both rich and famous. The College Board scores show that they have a great deal of intelligence, a considerable aptitude for both verbal thinking and mathematical concepts. They are handsome, healthy, bright-eyed, and alert, even charming. Does this mean that they arrive on the campus with a thirst for knowledge, eager for education, determined to be an intellectual? Some of our educators have assumed so over the years. They could hardly have been more wrong.

Twenty-five years in the practice of journalism have brought to me, more than to most men, an opportunity to view a wide range of the American scene. My observations over that period do not, let me say candidly, give me much hope for the future of intellectuality. Perhaps I should share with you some of my outstanding memories in this connection for the light that they will shed on the nature of the freshmen who arrive on your campuses.

I am reminded first of one of the richest men in America, a man who is on the board of directors of numerous important corporations, who runs a business of his own that intimately affects the life of one of our great cities. One evening this wealthy and influential man took me on a tour of his home from the basement, which, I found, contained a swimming pool, to the top story or attic, which contained a moving picture theater. There was not a single book in that house nor a single magazine except in his wife's sitting-room, which contained two or three of the newest women's magazines and a copy of *Life*. (*Life*, which has been kind enough to print most of my own articles in recent years, seems to crop up, thank goodness, almost everywhere.) Is chess an intellectual pastime? There was a chess set in the house, but it turned out that this was never used. The owner and his wife did not play chess. The expensive ivory men were a decoration, like a piece of statuary. Is music an intellectual pastime? There was an elaborate hi-fidelity system in the house, with hidden speakers. The records played on it were also in the wife's sitting-room, and I discovered that she was fond of Frank Sinatra and Xavier Cugat.

Is this unusual? Not in my experience. I recall a New York hotel suite, leased on an annual basis by a Midwestern tycoon who frequently visits the East—four bedrooms, a giant living-room, a dining-room and a kitchen, four radios, three television sets, a magazine rack full of old *Reader's Digests,* and three or four best sellers sitting on a table (still in their dust jackets, not very good books to begin with, and obviously untouched).

I recall the mansion of another industrialist, a man whom all of you would recognize immediately if I spoke his name, a man who, incidentally, has served on several government commissions and has quite a reputation for statesmanship. This was a truly beautiful country mansion with an outdoor swimming pool, bathhouse, and innumerable cottages for servants and guests. In the main part of the house, not a single book. In my guestroom, when I retired, a single volume provided for such guests as might prove to be intellectual—Edgar Guest's poems.

Perhaps I seem to be beating a dead horse here, for we hear a great deal nowadays about America's anti-intellectualism. But let me hasten to explain that in my opinion this is by no means just an American problem, nor just an American defect. In fact, to talk about American anti-intellectualism, I think, is to miss the point completely. Anti-intellectualism exists in all countries, and it has existed in all countries at all times. Most of mankind's progress, it is safe to say, has been made over the violent objections of the majority of mankind and by men and women who were despised and feared by the majority. The world has never been safe for the intellectual. The intellectual has always been an outcast, a freak, an object of fear and derision.

When we talk about America's anti-intellectualism, we minimize the problem. We say, in effect, that we are dealing with an accidental phenomenon limited to our own nation, and probably a temporary phenomenon limited to our own time. Neither of these things is true. We are dealing with one of the eternal millstones that mankind wears around his neck. We are fighting what in the world of the mind is the equivalent of those ancient scourges like heart disease and cancer and arthritis in the world of the body. The campaign to acquaint the student with the intellectual life of the college campus is no passing American need or American fad. It is a campaign which mankind, if it is to survive, will have to wage now and forevermore in every country on the face of the earth.

To put the problem in its proper perspective, and to give it its proper importance, we should, perhaps, turn the words around somewhat and state the facts like this: even in America, which has a higher level of general education than any other country in the world's history, we still do not have an atmosphere conducive to the creation or the functioning of the intellectual. Our "best" homes do not incline their children to intellectual pathways, and our wealthiest social groups favor skeet over Shakespeare and horsemanship over Horace Mann.

And now, just in case I haven't already discouraged you enough, let me talk briefly to you of another of the very serious problems which you face. This is the fact that the college freshman, alas and alack, is eighteen years old. What a tragedy this is—what an utterly impossible handicap—for those of you who are attempting to lead him up the road of intellectuality!

It takes a long time for the human brain to develop to its fullest capacity, a lot longer, unfortunately, than it takes the human muscular or glandular system. Boys and girls of high school age are sufficiently mature to win Olympic medals in athletics. They are also sufficiently mature, as we have seen in recent years, to marry and have children. But at what age do boys and girls become able really to appreciate a writer like Shakespeare or a teacher like Socrates; at what age can they really understand the principles of a social science or the full implications of the marvels of physics and mathematics? Most of you here know the answers to these questions much better than I; I shall venture only an informal guess that the very brightest boys and girls might achieve some sort of intellectual capacity at fourteen or fifteen, that the reasonably bright might do so at sixteen, and that the average boy or girl who is going on to college would not have this ability until the age of seventeen or eighteen. Think what this means. It means that when these boys and girls arrive at the college campus, most of them are just beginning to possess the ability to think. Yet during the period when their brains were growing up, life went on. We didn't just keep them in cold storage for those eighteen years. They were alive and kicking all that time, and learning too. We adults, who especially in America devote tremendous amounts of time and money to our children, set up activities to keep them busy and to teach them. They have learned a lot in their eighteen years. They have been subjected to all kinds of influences. They have been carefully trained and molded in many different directions.

At a very early age the schoolboy comes under the influence of the adults who run the local Little League, who teach him a good deal about the joy and importance of baseball and some of the principles of sportsmanship—not often including, I fear, the principle that what really matters is how you play the game, not whether you win or lose. He becomes a boy scout, and learns that a man's worth is measured by his ability to start a fire without matches and make a bed of pine boughs. Schools give parties for him in the evening, at which he is taught social dancing. In other words, we adults, for most of the eighteen years of his life before college, are stuffing him full of the importance of athletics, out-doorsmanship, and the basic box step invented by Arthur Murray.

Your beginning freshman not only comes to you ninety-nine times out of a hundred from a home and from a social background where the role of the intellect has been minimized, but also comes to you with a mind and character shaped by from fifteen to eigh-teen years of active life lived while his mind was quite immature. Intellectually speaking, these freshmen are babes in arms. At best they are mere toddlers. They have so much to learn, and, alas, to unlearn. I once wrote an article for the magazine of my alma mater in which I expressed the opinion that boys and girls of eighteen, even if their IQ's were 180, could not just be turned loose in a library and expected to learn. I said that they had to be shown the way to the library and even which way to turn the doorknob. Judging by the response to that article, a great many teachers with practical experience with eighteen-year-olds fully agree.

It is because of our failure to admit this fact, I think—for the lack of people like you who were willing to grapple with it—that American education has been a failure in the past. For I believe we have to admit that American education *has* been a failure. At least it has been a failure in terms of what it might have accom-plished. In no other country, at no time in history, has such a high proportion of a nation's youth been privileged to receive so much education. This means that we have had an unprecedented oppor-tunity to build an intellectual society—to take all the fine minds that would have gone uncultivated in other nations and in other times, and to start them marching up the high road to the moun-tains of pure reason. Heaven only knows how many brilliant minds have been wasted in the world's history for lack of someone to teach them to read and write. Even in twentieth-century Amer-ica, to our great discredit, we still let many brilliant students drop out of school for one reason or another, but we do keep a higher proportion of them in the classroom for a longer period than ever before. Thus, we live today in a nation which, according to the latest census report, has eight million college graduates, an unprecedented number, and millions more who have had part of a college education, adding up to a truly remarkable number of people who have been exposed to the campus atmosphere. Yet surely no one would claim that we live in an intellectual climate. Our popular institutions like television, radio, the average newspaper, and the average city may reflect a high degree of culture. All too often when you meet a man, you might guess from his position in the business world or his profession that he is a college graduate, but you could never guess it from his conversation, from his reading habits, or from his spare time activities.

Why is this? Well, as I see it, there can be only one possible reason. The reason is very simple. The colleges of America have been content to produce an inferior intellectual product. They have been afraid in the past to tackle the problem that you people are tackling here at this conference because the problem has seemed too difficult, too hopeless of accomplishment. Let me give you a homely and quite nonintellectual analogy. A few weeks ago I took my son to his road test for a driver's license here in New Jersey, and there I learned how the sovereign State of New Jersey judges whether a driver has learned enough to get his diploma, so to speak. The road test is not taken on a road at all. It is taken on a totally artificial and trafficless series of make-believe lanes, make-believe parking places, and make-believe stop signs. An examiner sits next to the youngster while he drives through this imitation world, and puts little marks on a chart that purports to break down driving into its essentials. There is one category marked turning, another marked backing, also stopping, starting, and so on. In each of these categories the examiner puts a mark that indicates superior, adequate, or inferior. Well, this, you see, is the bureaucratic way of testing a driver. It reduces the whole thing to a formula. No inferiors on the chart, and the prospect automatically passes. Enough inferiors, and he is automatically rejected. The system is absolutely safe, sound, and foolproof—and it tells absolutely nothing about the driver's skill. You know, and I know, and presumably the governor of New Jersey knows, that the only way to tell whether a driver is any good or not is to sit beside him for five minutes fighting through city traffic and then for another five minutes barreling down a turnpike. But to do this, you see, calls for subjective judgment, an anathema to the bureaucratic mind.

We have done something of the same sort in our colleges in the past; indeed, we have done so far too often. We have attempted to set our students down in the classrooms, throw a certain number of facts at them, and then judge them by how many of the facts stick —often measuring this by a true-false test, which has been the perfect corollary to the driver's test I mentioned. A true-false test is perhaps the ultimate in academic bureaucracy. For in these tests we abandon all pretense of setting our own standards for our graduates. We let them set their own standards. When ten students sit down and take one of the tests—at least this was the formula in my day—the bottom one was flunked and the top one was elected to Phi Beta Kappa. It did not matter a bit whether they were all Einsteins or all near morons, for we didn't care how well they could drive on an actual highway; we were only interested in how they could take the artificial curves of that isolated little practice ground. We taught them and judged them by formula, and spared ourselves the wear and tear of thinking. We failed to guide them; we did not really try to make intellectuals out of them; we did not even try very hard to teach them anything. We gave them a few facts and a few textbooks and then relied on them to do the learning by themselves.

Now I know that in the attempt to remedy these omissions of the past, you pioneers face considerable opposition in your task. I know that a great many of the most influential professors and administrators on the American campus wholeheartedly believe that we cannot lead our students, that the students must learn to lead themselves, that the young man or the young woman who does not become an intellectual by spontaneous combustion will never become an intellectual at all. I appreciate the idealism of these educators, but I deplore their lack of observation. They simply have not understood the nature of their problem. They have not realized the elementary fact that their students come to them from an unintellectual and even an anti-intellectual background, and the fact that the students are so terribly young, so callow, so unsophisticated in the ways of the mind. To the American campus in the past there has come—there still comes—many a boy fresh off a Mid-western farm, the son of a father and mother who never went past third grade, the product of a home that did not contain a single book, or a single magazine, or any newspaper except the country weekly from the nearest town, a boy graduated from a local high school forced to hire the least desirable 1 percent of all available American schoolteachers. At the opposite extreme, a few students have come to the campus who are the sons and daughters of Ph.D.'s, who grew up in homes that were full of good books and stimulating conversation, and yet who, in many cases, had rebelled against their parents, as adolescents often do, and thus were no more adequately equipped to acquire an education for themselves than was the ignorant and underprivileged farm boy. These stu-dents, both the farm boy and the rebellious scion of an intellectual family as well, might have IQ's at the 200 level. Yet unless they received some guidance, unless somebody told them what college was all about, unless somebody started their footsteps in the right direction and guided them by the elbow long enough to make sure they continued in it, they were almost certainly doomed to fail to become intellectuals in any sense of the word—and the chances were that they might even flunk out of school in the first six months.

The American educational philosophy has taken some strange twists and turns in the past. At one time we were classicists, who thought that if we taught a boy and girl—no, we did not even try to teach girls in those days—if we taught a boy sufficient Latin and Greek he would forever thereafter be able to solve all the intellec-tual problems with which he was confronted, including, presum-ably, the problem of how to live with a wife who had never studied either of those languages. More recently we have gone through a period when we were extreme pragmatists, and when many schools seemed to think they could fulfill their intellectual duty to civiliza-tion by teaching physical education and basket weaving. We know now from sad experience that both these philosophies were failures —utter, total, and complete failures. Some of you, thank heaven, know why. You have thought the problem through and have come to realize that the student who comes to your campus is not some preformed seedling easily and happily purchased from some mail-order house, which you can simply plant in a well-ventilated, well-fertilized, and well-watered library and watch grow, without further ado, into a fully developed and complete intellectual. You know that, on the contrary, the student is simply a human being, from an all-too-human background, and that, besides this, he is pathetically and almost hopelessly young. He is not a seedling at all. Being much more complicated than any form of vegetable life, he is more like some exotic and very delicate egg, which must be fussed over, handled gently yet firmly, and kept at exactly the right temperature for the exact number of days. It isn't easy to hatch an intellectual. If it were, we should have hatched a lot more of them in the past. But it is among the world's most noble tasks, if also among the most difficult, and if you succeed at it you will have been the foster parents of a far brighter world than the one in which we live today.

DESCRIPTIONS OF SPECIFIC ORIENTATION PROGRAMS

Williams College, University of Massachusetts, Hofstra College, Amherst College

Williams College

WILLIAM GRAHAM COLE, *President, Lake Forest College; Former Dean of Freshmen, Williams College*

Before describing the orientation program that was introduced at Williams a year ago, I want to say a few words about the considerations which led to its development.

In academic circles, we are constantly making curricular changes in order to do a more effective job. One of the wiser professors I know once made the comment that almost all this tinkering with the curriculum is futile unless students are really motivated to pursue it. If students are really motivated to study, almost any curriculum will work pretty well; however, if they are not motivated, almost no curriculum will work at all.

Virtually all freshmen arriving on college campuses in the fall are extraordinarily pliable; they are susceptible to the pressures and patterns they find there. They want desperately to belong; they want to be a part of the campus community. Thus, the whole orientation program is exceedingly important because it sets the tone, establishes a level of expectancy, and lets the freshman know at once what it means to be a student at this institution. If the orientation program is heavily weighted with advertisements of social and athletic activities, the freshman naturally gets an extracurricular image of the institution. On the other hand, if the orientation program emphasizes academic activities and intellectual opportunities, the freshman gets a much different image of the institution.

For some time, we had felt that there was something wrong with the conventional orientation program we were running at Williams. It was very much like some of the programs that Mr. Jenkins described yesterday afternoon. It included tours of the campus, an introduction to the library, impressive welcomes, and speeches about the importance of liberal arts education, which, incidentally, struck me as rather like the record I heard of recently, "Music To Listen to Mozart By." A year ago, we simply abolished all these tours and speeches on the assumption that the students were old enough to find their way around the campus and that they were able to use the library *in ambulando,* that is, in the course of their studies. We tried to place the whole emphasis of the orientation program on the intellectual life and to welcome freshmen at once to the house of intellect.

On July 1, we sent out a list of five books to the incoming freshmen. We deliberately avoided the "great books," feeling that they might bore incoming students and, thereby, defeat our purpose. Instead, we chose five lively, contemporary books which we thought would stir up some controversy. The five books that we chose the first year were selected from a group of twenty-five or thirty recommended by students and faculty alike. They were *The Ugly American* by Lederer and Burdick; *The Affluent Society* by Galbraith; *Apes, Angels and Victorians* by William Irvine; *Elizabeth The Great* by Elizabeth Jenkins; and an English novel entitled *Lord of the Flies* by William Golding. The last book provides the basis for a wonderful discussion in an orientation program, for it is a tale about a group of English schoolboys who are evacuated from England during World War III and dumped on a tropical island with no adults. It is a beautiful story that, like an onion, can be peeled and peeled, for it has many layers of symbolism.

As we suspected they might, many of the parents also read the books during the summer. This possibility limited our choice somewhat, for one of our faculty members was strongly urging us to select Mary Renault's *Last of the Wine,* which I also happen to think is a fine novel. However, since one of the themes of the book is male homosexuality, I was wary of our parents' getting hold of that and wondering what we were trying to orient these young men to.

When the freshmen arrived, we had a series of four panel discussions on successive days with two members of the faculty and two students on each panel. All eight of these students were members of Phi Beta Kappa; they were bright and articulate men with ideas and the ability to express them. We hoped these students would serve as Exhibits *A* through *H* of what a Williams man is like.

After an hour or so of panel discussion on one of the books, the freshmen returned to their dormitories, where they held their discussion under the leadership of their faculty adviser and two junior advisers, who were hand-picked for this particular function. Again, the good student was given prestige and status and held up as a kind of model to the freshmen.

There were some unexpected and valuable by-products of this program. In the first place, the faculty advisers got to know their freshmen better in these first four days than they had previously done in the entire first semester. They got to know the students' names, what they thought, and what made them tick. In the second place, the general level of conversation among the freshmen was raised from the trivia of "whom do you know and where are you from" to something of real substance that was worth talking about. But, most important of all, the student who was given real prestige and status was not the social lion or the athlete, but the student with ideas and the ability to express them clearly. These upperclassmen obviously impressed the freshmen and actually raised the level of expectancy of the whole freshman class.

The orientation program is only one tiny step in the direction of introducing the student to the intellectual life of the college, and it alone cannot create an intellectual climate. But, if the freshman's first step is in the right direction, it is certainly an auspicious beginning. All of us, students and faculty alike, who participated in this experiment at Williams feel that it has been successful and that it is worth continuing.

University of Massachusetts

SHANNON McCUNE, *Provost, University of Massachusetts*

The University of Massachusetts program for entering students has the same objective as other programs: to introduce the university to the students. This is important from our standpoint, for most of our freshmen are visiting the campus for the first time, and 25 percent of them have never been as far west as Amherst. Since we are eighty miles west of Boston, I suppose we ought to have an "Occidation" program rather than an orientation program for this particular group. (You have probably heard about the Korean student who asked during orientation week why *he* wasn't being oxidized!)

Another objective, of course, is to introduce the student to the university. Perhaps this is the major task, to get the student to understand what a university is all about.

We used to have the razzle-dazzle type of orientation program in which the sophomore honorary societies played the major roles. The freshmen learned primarily the college cheers and the school songs and, before the whole process was over, probably met a dean. The tests were done in a very hurried fashion, not because there wasn't sufficient time, but because the minds of the students were on the next "event." It just wasn't a good program; therefore, three years ago, we changed it.

Interestingly enough, we changed it by administrative fiat. Although this is rarely done on a university campus, there was enough faculty pressure to justify it in this instance. We decided that we could save a whole year's time by not appointing a faculty committee to discuss the situation; so we just went ahead and did it.

Since the academic and personnel deans were enthusiastic about instituting a new program, we sent several people out to Michigan and down to Penn State to steal any ideas we could get from them. As a result of this, our program contains modified versions of the Michigan State and Penn State programs. Our own three years' experience, of course, has led to additional changes, at least one of which resulted from asking some of our students what they thought about the program. After one student informed us that the word "welcome" had been used fifty-six times in two and a half days by various speakers, the word was practically banned! We have modified the program in other ways, and I know that this conference will give us other ideas, as it already has done, for still further changes.

Our orientation program is held nine times during the summer, usually from Thursday through Saturday; however, we also have one Wednesday through Friday session for orthodox Jewish constituents. We bring the students to the campus in groups of about 200, letting them choose the dates as far as possible. At the end of the summer, of course, we have to have one unscheduled, cleanup session just before Freshman Week (actually, the two days before registration).

Each session starts off with a talk by the president or the provost and an explanation of the program by the director of guidance. By 11:00 A.M., the freshmen are taking their tests, which include the American Council on Education Psychological Examination. The machines whirl during the night, and lists are posted the next morning for advanced placement examinations. Those who have done well on the English examination, for example, write an essay to see whether they can qualify for advanced placement in English.

Thursday night, the dean of men talks to the men, and the dean of women talks to the women. I am not sure what happens at these sessions, but I am sure that they are useful in acquainting the freshmen with the student personnel deans and the living conditions in the dormitories.

On Friday morning, in addition to taking advanced placement tests, the freshmen meet the deans of their respective colleges or schools. (We have ten colleges and schools.) In the afternoon, they meet their temporary faculty advisers, who sit down with them individually to discuss the test results and help them plan their schedules. Friday evening, we have a coeducational program in the women's recreational building. This includes swimming and other activities and is quite a bit of fun.

On Saturday morning, those who need to take more tests do so; those who were tied up in advanced placement tests on Friday register for their courses. At 10:30 A.M., we have a Parents Seminar, which includes a welcome by the president and a talk about the aims of the university by a senior faculty member. The parents, the students, and the faculty advisers then have lunch together, after which the parents are given the results of the tests. Finally, to conclude the program, the dean of men and the dean of women meet with the parents.

What are the good and bad features in this program? One good feature is that it is related very definitely to the academic life of the university. The program is run by the deans of the colleges and schools, and it emphasizes academic affairs, not extracurricular and peripheral activities. The first thing the student sees is the academic side of the university.

Another distinct advantage is the Parents Seminar, which, frankly, was an afterthought. Originally, we thought it would be a good idea just to have the parents come to the campus to pick up the students; so we sent out invitations, expecting only a few would come. For every 200 students, we now have 400 "parents," including grandmothers, aunts, and uncles for some of them! Since most of them have never been on a campus, this is their first "college" experience. It has real value.

As a state university, we are quite different from Amherst College, at the other end of town. Whereas about 85 percent of the parents of Amherst students have gone to college, only 15 percent of the parents of our students have attended college. Very often, therefore, both our students and their parents have a more serious adjustment to make. To ease the wrench a little bit, we make sure that the parents know what is going on, what a faculty member looks like, and what an institution of higher learning is trying to do. Enlisting their understanding and support is very worthwhile.

Another good feature of this program is our follow-up on the tests. We send the test results to each student's high school, and we also use the results to present a profile of the incoming class to our new faculty members as part of their orientation to the university. Later on, of course, this profile is presented to the entire faculty at one of its regular meetings.

Since we don't have enough money for an extensive professional counseling program, we rely on faculty members as well as on junior and senior students for various kinds of assistance. Although this system has many advantages, it has one obvious fault. Faculty members are miserable clerks. They don't follow the rules, and they arbitrarily postpone course requirements for some students. Since they take the large, intellectually oriented view, they have a disdain for requirements. Therefore, we often find the registration forms have to be worked over later by people who really know the regulations. This system has its disadvantages, but it purposefully involves the faculty in the program. A greater disadvantage is that we don't have a close faculty follow-up. Since there are not enough faculty persons available, students may be assigned to different advisers from the ones they had in the summer. This is a weakness we need to correct.

These are some of the problems we have. What are our dreams? I have picked up some good ideas during the course of this conference. For example, I like the idea of using a summer reading list and having discussions of the books in the fall. As a result of our discussions here, I see other possible ways to relate Freshman Week to the aims of our total university program. We shall certainly make a great many changes as we move ahead.

Like other large and growing institutions, the University of Massachusetts has tremendous responsibilities and opportunities. Because of size, we *have* to develop new programs. Because of changing conditions, we *can* develop new programs. Necessity will, therefore, again become the mother of invention as we are forced to discard old habits and discover better ways of doing things.

Hofstra College

RANDALL W. HOFFMANN, *Dean of Students, Hofstra College*

Hofstra is a young college (founded in 1935) in Hempstead, Long Island, more than 90 percent of whose students live within easy commuting distance of the campus. Located on a 70-acre campus about 25 miles from New York City, Hofstra has a full-time enrollment of slightly more than 3,000 and a part-time evening enrollment of over 5,000. It is a private, nonresidential college serving a typical, rapidly growing suburban community of approximately 1,500,000.

Hofstra students come, for the most part, from middle-class and lower-middle-class families, but a generous number also come from both the upper and lower extremes. They are predominantly "first generation" college students: 60 percent of the fathers and 77 percent of the mothers have had no college experience. More than 20 percent of the parents are foreign-born. In a relatively high percentage of the families both parents work full time. This is the picture of our college.

In the light of these facts, it should not be too surprising to learn that the parents of Hofstra students think largely in terms of the prestige value of the degree and the vocational value of higher education. Since all but 10 percent of the Hofstra students live at home and are constantly influenced by the values and aspirations of their parents and since Hofstra is philosophically committed to the liberal arts, the college has considered it desirable to establish not only an orientation program for students but also an orientation program for parents. The latter program will *not* be described in this paper.

The foundation for the present freshman orientation program was laid down ten years ago. It was preceded by a mistake. Very early in the short history of the college, a need was felt for something more than the usual Freshman Week, and the result was a course called "Effective Thinking," which was conducted under the auspices of the Philosophy Department. This course shared the fate of most departmentally aligned orientation courses and became just another philosophy course. It lost its all-college identity and became content-centered rather than student-centered. In establishing the present course, college authorities avoided the pitfall of departmental alliance by putting it under the aegis of the dean of students' office and by drawing its teachers from every department in the college. Simply, unashamedly, and unfortunately, it was called "Orientation."

Required of all freshmen, it is a one-semester course which meets two hours per week and carries two semester hours of credit with a final grade. Maximum enrollment in any class is seventeen. Throughout the first semester and part of the second, the instructor acts as the personal counselor for each individual in his class, gets to know each student exceptionally well, and writes a counseling report on each at the end of the year.

The salient feature of the Hofstra program, it seems to me, is its firm philosophical commitment to attitude change rather than to information giving, geographical orientation, or study of a fixed body of subject matter. Behind this commitment lies the conviction, shared by most college teachers, counselors, and administrators, that a student's receptivity to college and intellectual experience is not necessarily governed entirely by his potential. Many students of high potential, we know, do not get all that they should out of college, and many students of average or above-average potential get almost nothing at all. The job of orientation, as we see it, is to try to increase the student's receptivity so that he will get out of college as much as his potential will allow. We feel that the receptivity of students to the college experience depends pretty much on their attitudes in certain key areas. These attitudes, depending on their nature, can either hinder or help the developmental process that characterizes true education.

As we all know, students may have negative attitudes toward certain courses: mathematics, English, foreign languages, or others. Such negative attitudes toward specific courses may very well be changed through the student's experience with an inspiring teacher or a stimulating classroom climate. Attitudes of a more general nature, however, seem to us to require more systematic attention. Although the list is not exhaustive, the following are some of the attitudes we have in mind: attitude toward the purpose of a college education; attitude toward the tools of learning; attitude toward authority; attitude toward peers; attitude toward parents and family; attitude toward self.

The orientation course at Hofstra is designed specifically and pointedly to attack negative attitudes in these and other areas. I hope that it is not necessary for me to defend this contention or to expand on it to any great extent. Obviously, the student whose motivation is strictly vocational, or the student who feels that he is at college merely to tread water until he is handed a degree, is not going to get as much out of college as most educators want him to. Let me, however, give one slightly extended example of what I am talking about.

It is hard to say nowadays what would be an ideally healthy attitude toward authority on the part of young people who are approaching maturity. We do know two things, however: (*a*) that in the day-by-day business of getting a college education the student is thrown into constant contact with authority figures of many different kinds—faculty, administration, parents, and some of his classmates—and (*b*) that a student's attitude toward these authority figures will either help or hinder his development toward intellectual and emotional maturity.

A common negative attitude toward authority is open or veiled hostility. Very few teachers can completely escape being a target for this attitude. Usually through no fault of his own, the teacher's status as an authority figure, no matter how "nonauthoritarian" he may be, makes him fair game for the arrows of a hostility that was probably engendered elsewhere.

It is possible, of course, for a student to dislike a teacher and still get an A in the course. It is considerably more likely, however, that a student who has hostile feelings toward a teacher will reject consciously or subconsciously what the teacher has to offer. The rejection may come in the form of laziness, procrastination, or a deliberate "to hell with it" attitude. Whatever form it takes, it is usually self-defeating and runs counter to the teacher's legitimate aims.

In any case a hostile attitude toward authority can severely limit a student's receptivity to vital parts of the college experience. If he is going to make the most of himself and of college, such attitudes must change. We contend that the main purpose of orientation should be to cultivate favorable attitudes, and we attempt to do this through group discussion and through the exploration of certain ideas and topics.

In an intensive training program that includes a three-day workshop in the fall and continued meetings during the first semester, we try to train our orientation faculty to conduct effective group discussion. Our training program is an effort to convince the teacher that he has two main jobs in the orientation classrooms: (*a*) to establish a climate that will be conducive to individual participation, and (*b*) to help the individual students to achieve insight, express feelings, and communicate thought. Our general philosophy is that the group-centered process is more effective in causing attitude change among its participants than is lecture, preachment, or advice.

Within a climate marked by acceptance, warmth, good will, and reasonable permissiveness, the orientation class discusses topics that are centered around the attitudes we wish to affect. The following is a partial list of the topics discussed:

1. What should colleges do for the individual?
2. What is meant by a liberal education?
3. Academic skills and techniques
   a) Study habits and study conditions
   b) The use of the library
   c) Preparing for and taking examinations
   d) How to take notes
4. The nature and function of cocurricular activities
5. Student-teacher relationships
6. Student-parent relationships
7. Morality
8. Personal goals

Other topics of import and concern to the class are discussed provided they are germane to the problems of orientation. To assist the teacher and student, there is a text entitled *Controversy*,[1] consisting of articles related to the topics discussed. The articles were selected primarily for their tendency to provoke discussion and challenge complacency. For the instructor, another book, *Small-Group Discussion in Orientation and Teaching*,[2] is used in the training program for the orientation faculty.

One other facet of the orientation program at Hofstra should be mentioned because it complements the course and achieves a further end that most of us would prefer not to see neglected. I am speaking of personal adjustment. The climate of the classroom permits the student to feel accepted, to make friends within the group, and to have an outlet for feelings that are better expressed than bottled up. Second, through individual counseling with the instructor, the student has another opportunity to air problems that the teacher may be able to help him solve and to get necessary information and guidance as he makes his way through his freshman year. If problems are brought to light that are beyond the teacher's counseling depth, he refers them to the appropriate person.

Finally, let me list a few of the difficulties encountered in the Hofstra orientation program. The faculty at large continues to look with some suspicion on this type of nonacademic course. Since it is different from the usual content-centered course, it is con-

---

[1] R. W. Hoffmann and R. Plutchik, *Controversy* (New York: J. P. Putnam's Sons, 1959).

[2] Hoffmann and Plutchik, *Small-Group Discussion in Orientation and Teaching* (New York: J. P. Putnam's Sons, 1959).

sidered unworthy of academic status by some. The fact that its purpose is entirely different from that of the usual academic course does not seem to matter. We find it difficult to train the ordinary faculty member in small-group discussion techniques and philosophy, since his usual leaning is toward the lecture, and his normal need is to be heard rather than to listen, to lead by direction rather than by indirection.

The connotations of "orientation" have worked to the disadvantage of the course, both with students and faculty. We have overcome that difficulty this year, I hope, by changing the course name to "Freshman Seminar."

An evaluation of the course is naturally difficult. We have given before-and-after attitude tests and have found, to our gratification, that changes have occurred. Extensive and intensive interviews with students show that where the teacher has mastered the group-centered process, the attitude of students is highly favorable to the course. Nevertheless, total evaluation has necessarily remained, as it has with most other courses, primarily subjective.

Amherst College

EUGENE S. WILSON, *Dean of Admission, Amherst College*

There is one problem in being anchor man. By the time the baton gets to you, the race with time is won or lost. In this case I am afraid it has been lost, for I have very little time left and cannot possibly give you a full description of the Amherst orientation program. This is unfortunate, because it is so very successful. When our students leave the orientation program and go to classes, they have no personal problems; they have no feeling of antagonism toward the faculty or administration; they understand their position in their peer group and their relationship to their parents. Our psychiatrist goes away for a year, frustrated by lack of prospects!

There are two points, however, that I do want to touch on very briefly: (1) You can't run an orientation program without knowing what the expectations of your freshmen are. If you don't know what hopes and desires freshmen are bringing to your institution, you had better find out. You have built up expectations through your literature and through your admission representatives, and you had better find out if what you are doing matches what they expect because, if it doesn't, you will have an orientation problem. (2) I think college should be presented to a student as an opportunity, no more and no less, to learn as much as he is capable of learning. Prestige, if it exists, is not transferable. There is nothing magical about being in any particular institution. Nothing happens to a student unless he makes it happen. This point should be emphasized to freshmen.

Also, in talking to freshmen, it is important to remind each one that his rank in class is not going to determine his worth as a person, nor his success in later life. Each student has one responsibility and one opportunity—to use his own talents fully. The college exists to help him do this. For one student, this means one thing; for another, it means something else. Each has a place, and each has a worth.

Hopefully, in an orientation program you can show that learning is fun—not necessarily romantic, but fun. Learning will be romantic to only a few, but learning can be fun to almost every student. At the same time, it can increase his knowledge and understanding. Therefore, somewhere in the orientation program, a teacher ought to show how learning lifts the veil of mystery and often reveals interesting things.

The best orientation talk I ever heard was given by one of our English teachers. At the beginning of the orientation program he read a twelve-line sixteenth-century poem. He then asked the freshmen to read it. Finally, he asked, "What does it mean to you?" No one raised a hand. It had no meaning at all. Then he proceeded to tell them that this was a sixteenth-century marriage hymn. He told them about the customs of the sixteenth century, about the writers of that period, and about the vocabulary of that period. As he talked and began to unveil the background of this period, the poem suddenly had meaning. And when he had finished, he had dramatized beautifully how learning makes things interesting and relevant.

This year, we had three talks in our orientation program on the unveiling of mystery—by a scientist, an English professor, and a musician. Each one showed how knowledge in his area illuminates something, gives it meaning, and makes learning worthwhile just for its own sake.

At Amherst we state that our educational program has no direct vocational utility at all. We tell students when we interview them that their education will not be directed toward any vocation but that, curiously enough, it will be the best kind of preparation they can have for anything they later undertake. We try to point out that they will be using the same mental processes all their lives. They will be observing, thinking, and communicating, and they can apply these learning skills to anything. Finally, we explain to them that the responsibility for acquiring these habits and skills is theirs, not the college's and not the teacher's.

If you don't continue your orientation program beyond the first five days, you are missing a bet. Ten days after college opens, many freshmen have a sick feeling in the pit of their stomach. They had not realized that other students were going to look quite so bright. Home is a long way off. You tell them that you understand they feel this way and that freshmen everywhere do.

You meet with them before the first marks come out and explain why the marking standards are so different from the marking standards in high school. You tell them what the marks mean. You have a chance to eliminate some of the foolish attitudes toward marks. You write to parents explaining the marking system, so that they do not call up their sons saying, "How come you're getting a C when you never got a C before in your life?" You help the student explain to his parents.

Ten days after Christmas you meet with the class again. You say, "This is the low point of the year"; you explain why, and you tell them what they can do about it. Just knowing that others are suffering helps them. Misery loves company. So, you help them over these low spots by meeting with them in a group and explaining what they can do about it.

Then, at the end of the year (if you haven't done this, try it) sit down on some hot July day when you are alone in your office and write a little personal letter to twenty-five freshmen picked from various ranges of academic achievement, with A, B, C, D, and failing grades. Say something like this: "I have been thinking over the past year and your experiences here. How closely did we meet your expectations? Tell us where we failed. What courses proved uninteresting to you? Your name will not be revealed in any of our reports, but tell us honestly how you reacted to your first year in our institution."

The first year I did this I got replies from 23 out of 25. They were the most fascinating letters I have ever received, and I gave them to the president of the college. Keeping the boy's names confidential, he took out the sections that dealt with each freshman course and sent these excerpts to the heads of departments. Some interesting discussions in departments followed these reports.

A teacher ought to know what his students think. Administrators ought to know how a college is meeting the expectations of students.

You have to follow up at the end of the year with some students to get an idea of their impressions of the institution that you told them was so wonderful, so great, and that would do so much for them. You have to find out whether you did anything or not, what you did, and particularly what you did that needs improvement.

DISCUSSION

Presiding: ALAN SIMPSON, *Dean of the College, University of Chicago*

CHAIRMAN SIMPSON: You will recall that at the opening of the conference Dr. Adams exhorted us to think of more effective ways to introduce the entering student to learning. He was followed by President Gross, who suggested one way to do it—by firing students with one's own enthusiasm for the "romance of learning." Yesterday we heard reports on the characteristics and attitudes of entering students, as well as viewpoints of a student, a faculty member, a counselor, and an administrator. Last evening, Mr. Havemann painted a flattering description of ourselves as lonely lighthouses in a fogbound world. This morning we have heard descriptions of specific orientation programs.

By now we know what our enemies are. There is the pressure of numbers, which in some degree complicates the job for all of us.

There is the pressure of utilitarianism, which treats learning as instrumental to practical ends. There are the social interests, which either divert the student from all concern with learning or induce him to treat it as an entirely incidental matter. Finally, there are the compromises, the paradoxes, and the ironies within colleges that detract from our intellectual life.

We have also been conscious of some ambiguity about the precise nature of our charge. Are we to assume that we have an intellectual life on our campuses and that the only problem is to think of more imaginative ways of introducing the student to it? Or should we begin by examining ourselves? I am enough of a realist to suppose that this is neither the time nor the place for fundamental self-examination. May I suggest, therefore, that we focus our discussion on ways of improving orientation.

PRESIDENT STRIDER: You may be interested in an experiment we tried at Colby, which is by no means the University of Chicago. Two years ago, we recognized a need to intensify the intellectual life of the campus and adopted a plan suggested by a student member of the committee on freshman orientation. Like the program at Williams, ours involves summer reading assignments. A couple of years ago we gave students MacLeish's *J.B.* and the Book of Job, and we asked them to consider the implications of both of these with respect to the problems of evil, suffering, and the like. Then, during Freshman Week, we had a faculty panel discuss these matters. The students participated and asked questions.

It worked well except for the fact that somebody got his signals crossed—the letter that went out to the incoming freshmen was never sent to the upper-class advisers of these freshmen! The juniors and seniors were horrified upon arrival to hear the freshmen discoursing so learnedly. The next year we turned the thermostat up a little bit and had them read five dialogues of Plato, as well as five of the epistles of Paul from the New Testament, and asked them to consider the contrasts of the Greek and Judaeo-Christian concepts of love and so on. This time, the upperclassmen were properly advised, and the faculty panel was more successful than the first one. It had the effect of telling the students before they started classes that this was an institution where we expected them to be concerned with ideas. It was a rude shock to some of the freshmen and awakened them to the fact that we did expect them, as Dr. Sanford put it, to change and to develop new intellectual perspectives.

BRUCE DEARING (*Dean, School of Arts and Sciences, University of Delaware*): At the University of Delaware, we do three things that may have some utility. First, we start the actual academic program and the regular classes during orientation week. Many students arrive at college with high expectations. If they find only a discussion of living arrangements and social events of various kinds, the edge of their enthusiasm may have worn off by the time they get to classes sometime later.

For example, we begin the freshman English course during the orientation week. By the second day, students have had their first regular class meeting of a required course. They have had assignments, lectures, and discussion meetings and are well launched in their academic program within the first week. We think this arrangement has worked fairly well, and we hope it may establish an effective relationship between the theoretical discussion of academic matters and the actual experience of learning something substantive.

Second, we continue orientation throughout the first semester. Since we can't answer effectively questions that students haven't gotten to the point of asking, we feel it is a mistake to try to tell them more than they really want to know before classes begin. To meet questions as they arise, however, we continue to meet with freshmen once a week. The students in each school meet with their dean or his designate. This course carries no credit or grade, and works reasonably well most of the time.

Third, in the planning and administration of this course, we try to enlist the interests, concerns, and experience of those who were recently subjected to it. A very good committee of sophomores is used each year to help plan the course, to improve what they had the preceding year. Over the years, these sophomores have given me a good many insights into what the freshmen are thinking, what they wished to hear, what they didn't want to hear, what approaches worked well, and what other things were a waste of time.

In general, I think we have to find some way of getting better feedback from freshmen while they are being oriented to college. If we can discover the questions on their minds and then answer those questions when they are paramount, we shall make real progress. For example, there are critical times to speak about grades, about homesickness, and so on. There are other times when these matters appear to be irrelevant and of little concern. Timing, therefore, is important.

CHARLES E. SHEEDY, C.S.C. (*Dean, College of Arts and Letters, University of Notre Dame; Member of the Commission on the College Student*): I think the successful introduction of entering students to the intellectual life of the campus depends almost entirely on the caliber of teaching they encounter in the freshman year, and I want to say a word or two about the use of graduate assistants as it relates to freshman instruction in large universities.

There are on every campus men of the highest and next highest rank who are excellent teachers as well as excellent scholars and who love to teach freshmen. These best men should be allowed to teach freshmen. They can do it in big sections of some courses, or in small sections of twenty to twenty-five if the subject matter makes this advisable.

Graduate students should be allowed to teach, but they should not be cut adrift and permitted to teach as independent producers, as faculty men teach. Graduate students should be supervised in their selection of subject matter, their methods, their grading, and their attitudes toward students. This means that in multiple-section courses where graduate students are used, there should be a faculty member appointed by the department head to supervise the graduate students in the course. The faculty member should be responsible for this instruction and have corresponding authority. It may be that in some of our institutions these arrangements for supervision are made but not carried out because department heads or faculty supervisors are too busy or not really interested either in freshmen or in the graduate student–teacher. Thus, supervision becomes a mere form. This situation is doubly unfortunate because it is harmful to freshmen and uninstructive to the novice teacher.

The graduate assistant should not be thought of as a "section hand" or as a person capable only of mere mechanics and routine.

His first contact with teaching should be in a subordinate capacity as a leader of a discussion group under a master teacher; nevertheless, at some point he should be allowed to teach a class on his own, for he needs to have at least a beginning experience in teaching. An intelligent and reasoned approach to the problem of the graduate student–teacher will help solve a lot of the problems we worry about.

Now let me say a final word about another matter. For a number of years, I have seriously considered instituting a summer reading list for entering students. Now that I see that some of the people here have done this so successfully, I am going to try to put in some kind of reading list next summer and to arrange in the opening days a seminar or discussion to cover that reading list.

ALAN COUTTS (*Dean of Men, Dickinson College*): For the last two years we have been trying something I haven't heard anyone else mention. We came to the conclusion that freshmen can absorb only so much in the first four days of any orientation program, so we decided to continue our program well into the semester. Last year, when we were not able to find enough teachers who could or would assume responsibility for this continuing orientation, one of our students said, "Why don't we use our resource people to teach selected upperclassmen to serve as discussion leaders for groups of freshmen?" That is what we are doing this year.

Tuesday nights the resource people meet with the discussion leaders (all juniors and seniors) and go over the plans very carefully with them. Two discussion leaders, a man and a woman, are assigned to each group of fifteen freshmen. On Thursday nights the discussion leaders meet with the freshmen at a regularly scheduled class period. Attendance is required, and the class lasts for eight weeks.

Although some of the sessions have not been altogether satisfactory and certain changes will have to be made next year, we have discovered several important things. First, the upperclassmen, who sometimes consider themselves all-knowing, have had to reappraise their own experiences very thoughtfully in order to be helpful to the entering freshmen. Second, freshmen will listen and talk more freely to other students, upperclassmen particularly, than they will to faculty speakers who discuss the same topics.

DEAN HOPWOOD: Would you tell us one thing more? What is the content of the material that the faculty leaders teach these upperclassmen?

DEAN COUTTS:* Some of the topics are fairly difficult. The most successful one we have had so far has been the concept of honesty, honor on the campus.

DEAN HOPWOOD: This is an attitude. Is the discussion intellectually centered? Are you using your faculty to train these upperclass students to lead content-centered discussions or attitude-centered discussions?

DEAN COUTTS: Both. For example, we have used material on how to study and how to prepare for examinations. This is certainly content.

DEAN HOPWOOD: Not in my language it isn't.

FRANK C. ABBOTT (*Assistant Dean of the University, Bucknell University*): I should like to urge that we push our attention beyond the two or three days that are traditionally known as Freshman Week or Orientation Week. At Bucknell, we have made some recent changes that we believe have brought about a desirable difference in the attitude of the freshman class.

Whereas the Hofstra approach is a highly structured one, ours is quite informal. A couple of years ago, we enlisted about sixty faculty volunteers to advise ten or a dozen freshmen each and to stay with these students as sophomores until they had selected their majors and were transferred to their major advisers. Beginning with the Freshman Week itself, we try to get these faculty members into effective communication with their advisees through a group meeting, which is followed a day or so later with small social gatherings in faculty homes. Later, after the six-week grading period, there are scheduled personal interviews. Through these meetings within the first eight weeks, the freshman and his adviser usually come to know each other well enough to discuss freely matters that are of importance to the student.

It does seem important that there be, within the faculty, for every student, some person who has a broad interest in the student rather than just a narrow concern with his work in Mathematics 201 or Political Science 103. Our advisory program represents a modest effort along these lines. Although it needs further improvement, it does illustrate another approach to the objectives we are discussing at this conference.

VICKI PROSCHEL (*Student, University of Rochester*): I think we can get carried away with orientation and with the idea of how much we can do for incoming students. On the one hand, we are trying to encourage incoming students to take responsibility for their own education and their own learning; on the other hand, we are trying to smooth the way for them and remove all the obstacles. Speaking from the point of view of the student, I think that most of the men and women entering the university want to take the responsibility for their own education. They don't want to be babied.

W. C. H. PRENTICE (*Dean, Swarthmore College*): The last two or three days, as I have listened to what other institutions are doing and to some of the exciting and thoughtful experiments other people are making, I have become conscious of how little we do at Swarthmore, and I have begun to wonder how our students ever get oriented at all! But they do, and I have been thinking this morning that maybe we have stressed too little in our discussions the great diversity among our institutions.

For one thing, our student body is more homogeneous than most, both in ability and in interests. We have an arts college and only an arts college; we don't have any vocational programs; we don't have people who are there for business administration, education, and so forth. We also have great homogeneity, I am sure, in the expectations of people who arrive on the campus. Unlike Hofstra, for instance, most of our students come from families where there have been other college graduates.

All of this undoubtedly makes our problem easier. Freshmen are introduced to the intellectual life of the college without formal orientation and without even paying conscious attention to it. For one thing, we don't have any freshmen dormitories; freshmen live with upperclassmen from the day of arrival. For another thing, we don't have any freshman courses. All the college courses are open to all classes. Most of the courses that freshmen enter include a good many sophomores, a few juniors, and an occasional senior.

Within each dormitory we have a couple of upperclassmen who are especially responsible for the general health, welfare, and academic adjustment of the freshmen. They report to the deans if they think there is anything needing more adult attention; but, by and large, they take care of the freshmen's problems. They try to catch the ones who are homesick, as well as the ones who don't know anything about how to study, and steer them to the right faculty member or other official.

A lot of these things are done informally. They are not part of an orientation week or any special program, but they probably could not be done the same way in another kind of institution. In a small homogeneous residential college like ours, we are able to put a great deal of responsibility on upper-class students for teaching the younger students what is expected, what is possible, and what is available. As a result, orientation takes place naturally, quietly, and effectively.

Despite the fact that we have not yet tried it, I am fascinated with the summer reading program, and I hope we shall have an opportunity to do something of this kind. I think its main effect, however, will be to start the students a little faster when they arrive rather than to affect their total adjustment to the college very much.

PRESIDENT STRIDER: I heartily agree with what Dean Prentice has said. We do represent, as I think we are all quite aware by now, many varieties of institutions. Regardless of the differences among our institutions, however, we all seem to agree that we want to introduce our students to the intellectual life as soon as possible, to demonstrate that learning is exciting, and to assure them that they will have hard work ahead of them.

Whatever device we invoke, I think we should try to set the academic standard high enough so that the incoming freshman will have to stretch a little to reach it. On the other hand, we don't want to set it so high that it is out of his reach or out of keeping with the intellectual life already existing on campus.

If we find that in setting academic sights high enough to make the freshman reach, we are also setting them higher than they actually are in the rest of the academic program, then we should be concerned not with freshman orientation, but with the intellectual life of the institution itself.

No college is immune from this kind of difficulty. We should bear in mind, therefore, not only the need to introduce freshmen to learning, but also the constant need to strengthen the intellectual life of the whole college.

DEAN WILSON: We have a program that is different. All our freshmen live together and take exactly the same courses, except for the foreign language. Every freshman takes calculus, physics, humanities, composition, and an introduction to social studies through European history. No one is excused from these courses. Everyone reads some great books. When students say, "I have read the *Odyssey*," we ask, "Have you ever listened to Brahms's *First* more than once? Why did you listen to it the second time?" We try to get them to see that in their freshman work they are not repeating an experience, though they may be repeating a course.

If our program has any success, it is because the student uses his knowledge from the very beginning. He doesn't store it up for the six-week or final examination. Each week in composition, he writes three papers, which are corrected, handed back, and become the material for the course. In history, instead of listening to romantic lectures on what history is, he is studying the impact of one culture upon another and reporting how these cultures reacted. In physics, he is listening to talks, discussing problems, reading from two textbooks, and working in the laboratory. He observes, experiments, and reports in a laboratory book that is not written out for him.

Sometimes a student doesn't use his knowledge in a creative way for such a long time that he begins to wonder why he is collecting notes and data. He doesn't do anything with them. When he is suddenly asked to use them, he is confronted with the problem of deciding what is relevant and hopes he will remember it. If our freshman program has any success, it is because a student must put his knowledge to work in writing papers and in solving problems right from the beginning in all courses.

DEAN GUSTAD: I agree with Dean Wilson. The instrumental concept of learning does not mean that a student should necessarily study to be a better bond salesman; however, it does mean that he should learn to do many more things, do them better, and find them intrinsically interesting. I am reminded of a remark that Professor Skinner of Harvard made last year at a conference held in Boston. Speaking of the real rewards of learning, he said that if a student in this country learns to say correctly in French, "Please pass the salt," he gets an A. In France, he gets the salt. There is a considerable difference. The instrumental values and rewards of learning are very important.

MR. MORRISSEY: All entering students do not salivate and develop an appetite for learning at the ringing of the classroom bell. Sometimes they have to be enticed even to look at the curricular menu, and their taste for various courses has to be cultivated and acquired. Like Pavlov's dogs, however, students respond very well to reward and can probably be conditioned to study under the right stimuli. At least they can be *encouraged* to study if they live in an environment that recognizes and honors scholarship.

At the University of Maryland, the president and the faculty invite everyone to the first convocation, to honor those students who have achieved outstanding academic records during the past academic year. Although this is only the equivalent of awarding varsity letters to the university's best athletes, it has a very stimulating effect. The armory is filled with faculty, students, and parents. It is an occasion when the importance of scholarship is acknowledged and a time when individual efforts are rewarded. Although it is merely a symbolic occasion, it would be easy to underestimate its effect in creating a climate favorable to learning. I think we should not overlook these simple devices which, if nothing else, at least put the image of the scholar on a competitive basis with that of the athlete.

DEAN HOPWOOD: Like many others here, I have undergone conversion during these two days to the idea of the summer reading list. When people read the same books, they have a basis for communication, a common denominator for discussion. I can see that this happens at Amherst, where the common core of studies continues throughout the entire first year.

In a very diverse student population, however, I do not see how we can keep the common interests alive and the general conversation going after the first few weeks. In a large state university, for example, it is useless to bring the students from the dental hygiene curriculum and the students from the liberal arts curriculum together, for they don't have anything to talk about. The liberal arts people aren't interested in teeth, and the dental hygiene students aren't interested in philosophical concepts except in rare instances.

This is a problem for which I see no solution—maybe there isn't any. I should like to know if anybody sees one beyond the idea of having everybody read the same books before arrival.

DR. McCUNE: It is an interesting historical fact that at the University of Massachusetts common culture was at one time provided by the curriculum and reflected in the president's talks to the student body and in his Sunday chapel talks. In those days, everyone on the campus was familiar with certain classics and the Bible. On most campuses, of course, this is no longer true.

One of our problems is that we are now segregated into ten schools and colleges, and we have to find some way for the dean and faculty of each college to select a series of books or experiences and make them generally meaningful. Since we are stuck with vocationalism, we have to liberalize it so that there will be a broader basis for communication among both students and faculty. Frankly, I am not very optimistic about how easily this can be done.

DEAN DEARING: Most good faculty members enjoy the opportunity to address students in other departments and schools, especially on a timely topic. Two years ago we seized upon the interest generated by the hundredth anniversary of Darwin and had as many people as we could read *Origin of Species*. We found that these students were very eager to hear geologists, geneticists, literary historians, psychologists, and sociologists in whose classes they were not, and probably never would be, enrolled. Since this experiment was reasonably successful in stimulating campus-wide discussion, we tried a similar series of talks on Freud last year.

These lectures are made available without examination and without grade to upper-class and graduate students with good records for one credit hour. This year they are reading about Southeast Asia and calling upon our linguists, anthropologists, and others as needed. A fairly large segment of the university population has shown a genuine and serious interest in this program, which costs us nothing except the electricity in the hall. Our faculty members have been eager to cooperate. If we run out of enthusiasm after five years or so, we shall try something else.

DR. McCUNE: This year, we have used the national election as a focus for general interest and discussion. We have had Senator Flanders and other visiting lecturers on the campus to stimulate further discussion and debate. It has, I think, raised the general level of conversation.

PRESIDENT COLE: One of the things that has always impressed me about Oxford and Cambridge is their rule that students must take a certain number of meals each term in the hall, where there is always a very high level of conversation at the dinner table.

C. P. Snow likes to tell about the time he was sitting at the high table at Cambridge. After he tried two or three times without success to engage in conversation the gentleman across from him, the dean whispered, "He is a mathematician. We never talk to him."

The fact remains, however, that the students at Oxford and Cambridge do educate each other to a large extent—just through good conversation. Except for a few places where all the students are clearly dedicated to the intellectual life and where orientation to it is unnecessary and irrelevant, we have to contend with a different peer culture. This is the thing that licks us again and again. We have a pretty good intellectual climate among the faculty in most of our colleges, and we have a pretty good intellectual climate among our most serious students, but the trouble is that in so many of our institutions these students are in the minority. We need to enlist these serious students in a kind of fifth column within the whole student body, and one of the most obvious places for this to be done is at the dinner table, where they can raise the level of conversation by discussing ideas, books, and current events.

It seems to me that our major job is to start a conspiracy with the help of our ablest students. We are all working away at the curriculum. We are all trying to make our courses more interesting, our teaching more exciting. Yet the thing we have to do is work away at this peer culture problem. This is really the main obstacle to overcome in trying to create a climate of learning on the campus.

M. SUZANNE TUOHY (*Assistant to the President, United States National Student Association*): I think we should also enlist the foreign students in this effort. Many of them could help a great deal in raising the level of conversation if they were given a real opportunity to do so.

DEAN CADBURY: This morning several persons spoke of enlisting the cooperation of the parents. I wouldn't want the conference to close without saying a word about this. On the one hand, you can argue that it is a very good thing to involve the parents because they can then cooperate with the college and bring an influence to bear on their children. This is probably very important in a large institution where most of the students live at home. On the other hand, in a different kind of institution with different students, it is often important for the students to make a clean break with their home environments and to strike out on their own. In this situation, the break from home might be made much more difficult by involving the parents. At least, there are times when parents, in the interests of their children, ought to stay away.

DR. McCUNE: Did I understand you to say that this break with the parents is a wonderful thing?

DEAN CADBURY: I think the break with the parents is necessary when students come to college.

DR. McCUNE: How do you break this tie? Do you just sever it, like that, or do you make some kind of transition?

DEAN CADBURY: The point is that when the student comes to college, it is often a very good thing for him to get away from parental influence. This is part of the process of growing up.

DR. McCUNE: Parents are still paying for it, and they still have a tremendous influence. If they don't understand what you are trying to do, and many of them do not, they exert a countervailing force.

PRESIDENT COLE: Personally, I think it depends on the particular situation; nevertheless, I think a little learning is a dangerous thing for the parents. Sometimes parents need to be told, "Now that you have turned them over to us, let us handle them. If they get into trouble, they may need tender, loving care. If so, we shall give it to them. If they need a good swift kick where it will do the most good, we shall give it to them. We are now in a better position to understand them than you are. They want love, acceptance, understanding, and support, no matter what, but go home and leave them in our hands."

DR. BROWN: President Cole's comments remind me of that famous remark by a Princeton president to an overly solicitous mother, "Madam, we guarantee results, or we return the boy."

LAWRENCE E. DENNIS (*Vice-President for Academic Affairs*

Pennsylvania State University): All institutions act in *locus parentis* to varying degrees; nevertheless, some of them have found that it is exceedingly worthwhile to counsel with parents. Parents very often have a complete misconception of what a college education involves and of what their son's or daughter's actual abilities are. Sometimes parental counseling is the only way to resolve a tragic conflict between a parent's career plan for his son and the son's own interests and abilities. Far from delaying the break with parental influence, these conferences with parents help the student gain his freedom, find his own way, and establish his own independence more quickly and much more satisfactorily.

WILLIAM L. DUREN, JR. (*Dean, College of Arts and Sciences, University of Virginia*): I should like to summarize briefly some of my impressions of this conference: First, it has deepened my skepticism of the effectiveness of the conventional freshman orientation program as a means of introducing students to the intellectual life of the college. Second, it has taught me some interesting things that can be done, including a few that I should like to adopt at our institution. But, most of all, it has impressed upon me the fact that what any orientation program can accomplish is, at best, limited.

As several people have observed, if there is a genuine intellectual life, the students will find it out; if there is no real intellectual life, the students will find that out, too. And, in the latter case, an artificial orientation program may only make matters worse, for it will raise expectations that cannot be satisfied. Thus, the problem really becomes one of creating and strengthening an intellectual climate throughout the entire institution.

Many good experiences have been shared here, and many promising ideas have been generated. But I think this is what I should like to take back to my university: a feeling of renewed confidence that all of us can do a lot more than we are now doing to improve the intellectual life of the *whole* institution *both within and outside the classroom,* not only for the freshmen but also for upperclassmen, graduate students, medical students, law students, engineering students, and everyone in the campus community. To me, this is a very attractive challenge.

CONFERENCE PARTICIPANTS

FRANK C. ABBOTT, Assistant Dean of the University, Bucknell University

ARTHUR S. ADAMS, President, American Council on Education

ANN FRANCIS, SISTER, Dean of Students, Trinity College, Washington, D.C.

ANNA CONCILIO, SISTER, Dean of Studies, College of St. Elizabeth

B. J. BORRESON, Executive Dean for Student Life, University of Maryland

PAUL J. BRAISTED, President, The Edward W. Hazen Foundation

ALLEN D. BRECK, Professor of History, University of Denver

NICHOLAS C. BROWN, Staff Associate, American Council on Education

HAROLD W. BROWNING, Dean, College of Arts and Sciences, University of Rhode Island

WILLIAM E. CADBURY, JR., Dean, Haverford College

WILLIAM GRAHAM COLE, President, Lake Forest College

ALAN COUTTS, Dean of Men, Dickinson College

K. PATRICIA CROSS, Dean of Students, Cornell University

BRUCE DEARING, Dean, School of Arts and Sciences, University of Delaware

LAWRENCE E. DENNIS, Vice-President for Academic Affairs, Pennsylvania State University

ALBERT I. DICKERSON, Dean of Freshmen, Dartmouth College

ELIZABETH DREWS, Associate Professor, College of Education, Michigan State University

WILLIAM L. DUREN, JR., Dean, College of Arts and Sciences, University of Virginia

WILSON H. ELKINS, President, University of Maryland

TERRI GALVIN, Executive Secretary, Intercollegiate Association of Women Students, Activities Office, San Jose State College

ROSE K. GOLDSEN, Associate Professor, Department of Sociology and Anthropology, College of Arts and Sciences, Cornell University

MASON W. GROSS, President, Rutgers—The State University

JOHN W. GUSTAD, Dean, College of Liberal Arts, Alfred University

ERNEST HAVEMANN, Author, 31 Abbington Terrace, Glen Rock, N.J.

JOHN R. HILLS, Director, Testing and Guidance, Regents of the University System of Georgia

ARTHUR A. HITCHCOCK, Executive Director, American Personnel and Guidance Association, Washington 9, D.C.

JOHN E. HOCUTT, Dean of Students, University of Delaware

RANDALL W. HOFFMANN, Dean of Students, Hofstra College

KATHRYN L. HOPWOOD, Dean of Students, Hunter College

TIMOTHY JENKINS, National Affairs Vice-President, United States National Student Association, 3457 Chestnut Street, Philadelphia 4, Pa.

J. W. LAMBERT, Dean of Students, College of William and Mary

DOROTHY J. LIPP, Dean of Women, Pennsylvania State University

T. R. McCONNELL, Chairman, Center for the Study of Higher Education, University of California, Berkeley

SHANNON McCUNE, Provost, University of Massachusetts

TONI McCUNE, Student, University of Massachusetts

M. GIOVANNI, SISTER, Dean, Georgian Court College

THOMAS MORRISSEY, President, Student Government Association, University of Maryland

JEANNE L. NOBLE, Assistant Professor of Education, School of Education, New York University

W. C. H. PRENTICE, Dean, Swarthmore College

VICKI PROSCHEL, Student, University of Rochester

NEVITT SANFORD, Professor of Psychology, University of California, Berkeley

AARON SAYVETZ, Professor of the Physical Sciences in the College, University of Chicago

ALVIN R. SCHMIDT, Director of Counseling; Assistant Dean of Men, School of Liberal Arts, Tufts College

JOSEPH A. SELLINGER, S.J., Dean, College of Arts and Sciences, Georgetown University

JOHN W. SHAINLINE, Dean of Students, Gettysburg College

CHARLES E. SHEEDY, C.S.C., Dean, College of Arts and Letters, University of Notre Dame

ALAN SIMPSON, Dean of the College, University of Chicago

GEORGE G. STERN, Professor of Psychology, Psychological Research Center, Syracuse University

S. TOWN STEPHENSON, Dean of the Faculty, Washington State University

ROBERT E. L. STRIDER, President, Colby College

LEILA A. SUSSMANN, Assistant Professor, Department of Sociology and Anthropology, Wellesley College

JUNE TOULOUSE, Student, University of Maine

M. SUZANNE TUOHY, Assistant to the President, United States National Student Association, 3457 Chestnut Street, Philadelphia 4, Pa.

EUGENE S. WILSON, Dean of Admission, Amherst College

W. MAX WISE, Professor of Education, Department of Guidance and Student Personnel Administration, Teachers College, Columbia University

RAYBORN L. ZERBY, Dean of the Faculty, Bates College

AMERICAN COUNCIL ON EDUCATION

LOGAN WILSON, *President*

The American Council on Education is a *council* of national educational associations; organizations having related interests; approved universities, colleges, teachers colleges, junior colleges, technological schools, and selected private secondary schools; state departments of education; city school systems and private school systems; selected educational departments of business and industrial companies; voluntary associations of higher education in the states; and large public libraries. It is a center of cooperation and coordination whose influence has been apparent in the shaping of American educational policies and the formation of educational practices during the past forty-three years.

X